# Shooting the Bull

a field guide to identifying political lies in real-time

# Guy Smith

**Free Thinkers Media**

# Free Thinkers Media

2360 Corporate Circle · Suite 400
Henderson, NV 89074

ISBN: 09-8324-070-1
ISBN-13: 978-0-9832407-0-9

Library of Congress Control Number: 2010943285

To Sweetpea – let this be the first of
endless adventures together.

# Foreword

Why does Sarah Brady lie?

One would not think it of her by appearance alone. Sarah's grandmotherly countenance reeks with such kindhearted sincerity that you can almost smell chocolate chip cookies baking in her kitchen. A war baby who came of age in Ike's 1950s, at first glance she appears to be the very hallmark of honorability – the type of person you would ask to sit with your kids, mediate a neighborly dispute or hold competing wagers on an illicit cock fight. Alas, her sincerity is supplanted by cynicism, the type that only baking canards can produce.

On the subject of gun control nary a truth can be found emanating from her lips. Her web site fumes statistical irregularities than cannot be explained by sloppiness or stupidity. Sarah's newspaper interviews echo grander, borrowed falsehoods. The organization that bears her name, the Brady Campaign, is a veritable misinformation factory employing a full set of machinery for minting political falsehood. Well, almost the full set. We have yet to see them produce a doctored photograph of Ted Nugent pumping a few rounds into Chuck Schumer.

Why then does Sarah Brady and nearly everyone else campaigning for gun control lie? For the same reason that men lie to their wives about matrimonial infidelity and politicians lie about ... well, everything. She is possessed with the same motivation as a jewel thief who lies to the police as they drag him away from a mansion. Sarah lies for the same reason as a street-corner drug dealer who slips crack junkies a homebrew of candle wax and baking soda, or as Michael Moore does when claiming not to eat children whole.

Sarah lies in order to gain something she could not otherwise acquire honestly. Sarah and her cohorts fib to achieve political ends for which they have fading public support and finance. Sarah and her minions propagate propaganda to take from you what the law says they cannot take. Call it the "do-gooder" syndrome, a disease in which blind fixation on correcting a perceived social ill makes rampant dishonesty a permissible tool. This Holy Cause – or Unholy Curse – that permits telling lies in order to change the world is easily observed and difficult to swallow. Not even the famous Stomach from Flint could manage to ingest it all.

Sarah is my proxy for everyone in the gun control industry who has bent a statistic, knowingly cited flawed studies or denied demonstrable fact. She is the gentle face that masks flagrant falsehoods spun by the Dianne Feinsteins and Josh Sugarmanns of the world. Sarah uses her grandmotherly façade as a distraction from the impassioned and equally fictitious rhetoric of Rebecca Peters, the Stalin-cast mistress of global gun control. Mrs. Brady is the lovable decoy for Clintonesque proclamations that "we don't want to ban guns."

Give that woman a cigar!

Being a normally charitable type, I loathe incriminating those who make simple yet honest mistakes. Were I on trial for such petty crimes I'd serve a little time. But through years of researching the gun control industry I have ruefully come to the conclusion that their misinformation is no mistake –

that Sarah and her comrades know the facts and avoid them like a Ted Kennedy Memorial Tequila Road Rally. In the scorched-earth warfare of political posturing, the battlefield is littered with the corpses of false proclamations lanced with the slow but sharp sword of evidence. Yet the gun control industry's mendacious modus operandi tirelessly launches soldier after soldier of fabricated fibs seeking to overwhelm opposition and the Constitution by the sheer bulk of fakery. I am told that Sarah has been approached by the estate of Joseph Goebbels, which sought to be mentored on effective propaganda techniques – the Goebbels estate wishes to make poor Joseph look credible by comparison to the gun control industry.

More fascinating than the perpetual production of misleading information by gun control forces is their mastery of every form of political mythmaking and policy positioning (or more accurately, repositioning, given their long losing streak and serial tactical retreats in the United States). For many years I have exposed and exploded gun control folklore through *Gun Facts*, the standard desk reference on gun control sophism. This tome – read in over 165 countries around the globe and cited in testimony before government committees – catalogs Sarah and Company corkers and fills the resulting craters with hard data. Through these efforts I learned that Sarah and associated syndicates could easily author study guides on the art and science of political misinformation.

So, I decided to beat them to the bookshelves. Thanks for the raw material Mrs. Brady.

*Shooting the Bull* is a twin-helixed survey of both the common forms of modern propaganda and specific gun control subterfuge. Each form of distortion is amply illustrated by case studies detailing what the gun control industry told the weary people of our planet and what pure equine effluvium it was. By the time you turn the last page, you will be gasping over how you have been deceived about guns, crime and most importantly the utter failure of the 20,000 gun control laws Sarah and her minions falsely fostered on America. Armed with this catalog of political myth manufacturing techniques, you will suck air recognizing how you have been misled elsewhere in public debate. Forearmed, you will be better able to detect biased bunk in the future.

Strap in Tiger, you're in for a bumpy ride.

# Foreword by Brian Patrick

In earlier centuries Guy Smith would have been designated a heretic and condemned to burn at the stake, unless of course he recanted. But after reading his book and having met the author, I don't believe him the recanting type. In any case, *Shooting the Bull* would certainly have been placed on the index of forbidden books.

Guy Smith – instigator and author of *Shooting the Bull* – is a citizen-intellectual of the New American Gun Culture. To social elites who wish to dictate laws and conditions by which we must live, the citizen-intellectual is the most annoying creature on Earth. Rather than going along with the program, the citizen-intellectual poses inconvenient questions. He points out logical fallacies, hypocrisies, self-serving lies, stupidities and factual inaccuracies. He satirizes. He is irreverent and non-compliant. In short, he does his own thinking. And then he goes and writes a book. You see how this critical thinking stuff spreads. No wonder elites hate and fear it.

Even before *Shooting the Bull*, Smith was well known as the writer of the influential e-book, *Gun Facts*, available online since 1999 as a public service, and which has informed numerous citizens, students and even the occasional journalist. This work established him as a pioneer in the innovative, alternative forms of media that the New American Gun Culture has used so successfully to inform and coordinate, thereby becoming a major political power to be reckoned with, instead of merely a target for elite administrative ambitions.

Smith embodies an informed type of American democracy that has been replacing the passive mass informational systems of past decades, when most people acquired opinions and knowledge from national news systems over which social elites exercised near total control. These elites designated lawful gun ownership and the citizens who owned guns as deviant.

Essentially the New American Gun Culture is a revolution against imposition of elite authoritarian power and thought control. This revolution has been conducted chiefly by means of independent critical thinking, by means of information. For critical thinking is fundamentally revolutionary because it challenges authoritarian power. Reading Smith's *Shooting the Bull* recalls a line by philosopher Michel Foucault: "The purpose of knowledge is to cut." In this book Smith doesn't merely cut, he systematically guts gun control propaganda, including its elite celebrity propagandists. Be prepared to see some pretty ugly innards and a few amputations.

Before reading this book in manuscript form (or meeting its author), I was told that Smith had an "acerbic writing style." Apparently this warning was provided out of fear that I might be a mild-mannered academic of such delicate sensibilities that I would be shocked by blunt and direct use of language. My academic colleagues are certainly shocked by Smith, to my delight, as I try some snippets on them. Smith disrespects, mocks, refutes and derides the mass-media-derived stereotypes that they unthinkingly accept as knowledge. He also makes dreaded *ad hominem* attacks, wherein one refers to an idiot or liar as an idiot or liar. Apparently there is some unwritten rule barring this practice in academia. My reaction to Smith is a very solid, "Yes."

My colleagues often mention the importance of imparting what they call "critical thinking" skills to college students. They claim their students will then go forth and meaningfully participate in American democracy as informed rational citizens, capable of separating truth from lies and reasoned argument from insubstantial claims.

And yet only rarely do I see any of my colleagues in the social sciences or humanities demonstrate anything remotely like critical thinking. Collectively, they tend to march in lock step. This is especially true concerning matters related to guns, gun laws, gun ownership, the Second Amendment and American culture generally. In fact, on the whole, when it comes to gun topics my colleagues are perhaps the most systematically misinformed (note that I did not say "uniformed") people that I have ever encountered.

How can people so highly educated, holders of Ph.Ds from prestigious universities, themselves part of the elite (or at very least its servants), be so misinformed? The sad fact is, contrary to what my colleagues believe about their state of social enlightenment as compared to lesser mortals, the highly educated are most susceptible to the type of information called *propaganda*.

Highly educated persons – I speak of formal education here – live in an artificial world of symbols, literature and information that becomes quite real to them over time, more real than anything else. They are not only exposed to the usual streams of mass-mediated propaganda – but they actively seek and consume much other information besides, absorbing quantities at second and third hand. All this is reinforced by their social environment made up of people much like themselves. They pride themselves on being seen as "informed."

*Informed by what however?* This becomes the important question. And because they spend so much time closeted with themselves, mirroring and echoing, looking to "experts" with whom they sympathetically resonate, they are suckers for the sort of dramatically simplistic explanations of the world that propagandists manufacture and disseminate. Typically, the themes of this anti-gun propaganda appear absurd or idiotic to people who have direct knowledge of guns or who have taken the trouble to genuinely inform themselves. Tens of millions of members of America's gun culture know that guns don't "just go off," that law-abiding people, both by nature and definition, are not subject to homicidal rages with firearms (or with any other instrument), and that guns are not germs that cause epidemic violence.

But these sorts of lurid explanations make a great deal of sense to most academics. By training, prone to a top-down communication style of social prescription of judgment, they seem to feel not only justified, but morally obligated to talk down to those whom they perceive to be below them. And they perceive legitimate gun owners to be far below them. In fact there is really no such thing as a legitimate civilian gun owner in academic cloud-palace sociology, where gun owners are viewed only as a social and moral problem.

Let me offer you a sample of how this works out in day-to-day life. While in graduate school at University of Michigan back in the 1990s I once wore a pair of camouflage cargo pants on campus. Immediately faculty and fellow grad students began to stare. To me these pants signified only comfort and thrift, but it soon became obvious that they signified something else entirely to these others. Referring to the militias then prominent in mass media news accounts, they would question me in accusatory tones, "What do you think of the blowing up of the Federal building in Oklahoma City?" as if they thought I approved of this outrage. There was talk about "your sort of people," meaning me. And all this was merely over a pair of suspect pants. So here the mental equation is camouflage pants equal mass murder. Or, a fellow grad student, now a professor at a state university, refused an offer to shoot a target pistol because, he said, "It's a moral thing." Gun use, even for target shooting, equals immorality. This person was telling me quite directly that I was his moral inferior.

Academics blurt out things like this all the time in my presence. The only reason I think I achieved tenure was because my colleagues, seeing that I published books on the subject of gun culture, and knowing that I professed on the subject of propaganda, simply assumed that these were anti-gun studies that exposed pro-gun propaganda. It apparently never occurred to most of them that any other intellectual approach was possible (nor did it occur to them to actually read my books).

So considering that on the whole America's professional academic intelligentsia – its pharisaical class – has flopped, who, then, propagates critical thinking regarding gun-related issues in American society?

Here we find a most encouraging social trend. Starting around 1970, American citizens began doing what they have characteristically done concerning critical thinking. Rejecting self-serving authority's attempts to impose negative interpretations on the meanings of guns and gun ownership, non-elite citizens began having unauthorized thoughts, a practice once called heresy. Pursuing their own lines of critical thinking on guns, they began to communicate these heresies. Another name for this is *revolution*. America's citizen-intellectuals especially rejected biased media coverage and oppressive legislative policies on firearms that had been informed by elite thinking. Since then we have seen a virtual American Enlightenment concerning guns and the meaning of the Second Amendment. All this has been achieved via that uniquely American schematic for social action – the First Amendment – through free exercise of thought, association and expression.

Independent pro-gun thought and scholarship such as Guy Smith's has bloomed over these past few decades. Gun culture's native intellectuals, its many autodidacts (thinking, literate, self-educated citizens, the best kind of citizens) and even a few renegade professors have discussed, published and flourished. These activists have been authentic "community organizers," forming a genuine discursive community, as opposed to lackeys sent by elites to herd rabble into voting blocks. Thus informed, numerous pro-gun citizen associations have commenced effective courses of social action. They transformed the old traditional gun culture of duck hunters and hobbyists into the politically charged new gun culture that exists today. Critically thinking revolutionaries back in the 1970s also changed a relatively sedate National Rifle Association from what had been essentially a hobby-group of shooters and collectors into the flagship of this new gun culture, and what is now perhaps the most effective political action group in the U.S. Had it not been for the exercise of true, unrestrained critical thinking, gun rights in this country would certainly have been legislated into oblivion. The gun rights movement has become both a political power and a source of knowledge.

Important to the subject of Guy Smith's book, denied meaningful access to the "official" national organs of communication by which social elites disseminated their anti-gun worldview, gun culture activists formed their own "anti-media" of communication. This was exactly what revolutionary thinkers in the Reformation and American Revolution did when they used that revolutionary new medium of their time – the printing press – to share their thoughts. To better inform and coordinate themselves, American Revolution thinkers formed Committees of Correspondence in the states. New gun culture intellectuals did much the same thing, creating new state-level groups and/or enlarging the sphere of action of pre-existing rifle and pistol associations. In the 1990s the new gun culture met computer-mediated-communication, the revolutionary media of modern times, and progress accelerated. Pro-gun blogs and web sites, e.g., Smiths's *Gun Facts*, are what pamphlets were to the American Revolution.

The result has been, well, revolutionary. Even a partial listing of successes of the new gun culture is too long to include here. Much restrictive anti-gun legislation has been successfully resisted, buffered or overthrown in the courts and in state houses. The right-to-carry concealed carry movement began in the 80s with Florida's law serving as a national template. With the advent of computer-mediated communication, right-to-carry acquired even greater social momentum. Whereas previously the right to licensed carry of concealed handguns for average citizens had been legislated out of existence in most states, becoming a privilege reserved for local elites (government officials and their brothers-in-law), now more than five million people are licensed to carry under these laws. It is a widely recognized right. Students have now organized, setting up their own media and online discursive communities dedicated to extending the right-to-carry to university campuses. Concealed carry has brought many women into the new gun culture along with other previously unaligned converts. Following on the successes of the concealed carry movement have been Castle Doctrine and Stand-Your-Ground laws recognizing citizens' right to armed self-defense of their homes and persons. With the *District of Columbia versus Heller* Supreme Court decision in 2008, the new gun culture has snatched back from elites the right to interpret the meaning of the Second Amendment as an individual right, despite the cloud-palace fantasy that it did not apply to individual citizens, but only to states. And ramifications of *McDonald versus Chicago* which will occupy court dockets for years to come, will certainly assure the full incorporation of the Second Amendment under the Fourteenth Amendment, nullifying unconstitutionally restrictive gun prohibitions in some states. With its mastery of anti-media, the new gun culture is numerically stronger than ever and still growing. While gun sales are up dramatically, violent crime is down. And all this has come about and continues through the application and sharing of critical thinking.

That Guy Smith goes beyond the merely acerbic is understandable. Indeed, he can be vitriolic in regard to the distortions, factoids and logical fallacies that continue to be regularly and willfully promulgated by national gun control organizations and their spokespersons. These organizations misrepresent themselves as citizen groups, a misrepresentation often picked up and repeated by mass news media, when they are in actuality small, top-down propaganda centers run by professionals who claim to speak on behalf of an abstraction they call "the public." This latter claim is nonsensical on its face because while at least several million (a very conservative estimate) Americans are formal, dues-paying members of new gun culture associations, the cumulative membership in *all* anti-gun organizations is no more than about 125,000 persons (very generously estimated – see *The Lie of Coalition*). Anti-gun organizations have no mass public support, just elite support and funding.

But what elites want, they will impose if they can, by any means possible. A proven method has been through top-down "communication campaigns," i.e., propaganda. Delivery is through misleading public relations techniques such as publicity (the creation or simulation of news), media relations, speaker bureaus, celebrity spokespersons and staged visually exciting events designed to garner mass news media coverage. Anti-gun groups are very good at using mass news media and have dominated the news for years. For an example, consider a series of "lay down and die" events orchestrated by the Brady Center, purportedly memorializing the Cho murders at Virginia Tech in which thirty-two anti-gun demonstrators, recruited for the occasion, dressed in black, lay down as if dead for three minutes to represent the number of people allegedly killed daily by guns, and how quick and easy it supposedly is get a gun. Therefore "loopholes" must be "closed." But Cho bought his guns legally well beforehand from licensed dealers after passing the Federal instant background check. It remains unclear how the above sort of instant melodrama connects either with the facts of the Cho murders or the non sequitur conclusion offered that "loopholes" must be closed. The primary "loophole" that the principals of anti-gun organizations really want closed is called the Second Amendment. These "lay down and die" events provide good ten-second visuals for the news, however misleading. But interpreting the real meaning of such events is what fact-based critical thinking is all about – illumination rather than dark deception.

Guy Smith's method throughout the book is to systematically debunk such misrepresentations, the *Bull* of his book's title, the standardized lies which gun control organizations and "advocates" traffic. He enumerates specific types of lies that gun controllers have used over and over again to distort truth. He supports his work throughout with vividly concrete evidence. Smith's *Lie of Definition*, for example, addresses the use of impossibly vague, poorly defined terms such as "assault weapon" frequently used by anti-gun politicians and mass media to mislead.

The book equates to a course on critical thinking. It also resonates with the uniquely American endeavor of *propaganda analysis* that began after the First World War. Americans realized that propaganda had poisoned the informational well of American democracy and that propaganda techniques needed to be analyzed and catalogued. There was a time in the 1930s when the Institute for Propaganda Analysis, since defunct, coordinated teaching of its "Devices of Propaganda" in more than 500 high schools. Perhaps our schools should emulate this effort today. Smith sets the example.

In common with other critical thinking reformers, Smith is highly irreverent. He is often outright rude, for his is the voice of invasive Reason. He calls out well-known people who should (and probably do) know better than to say and do as they say and do. In many ways he reminds me of Martin Luther, renegade priest (the academics of those times) and critical thinker who challenged widespread institutional corruption in the religious-political system of his era, thereby changing the course of history. Luther would also call people out by name, saying that an adversary "Has learned his A-B-C all the way down to B," and "I feel much freer now that I am certain the pope is the antichrist," a statement that could easily have gotten him burned.

Using this in-your-face approach, Smith commences his investigation by asking a damned good question, "Why does Sarah Brady lie?" He castigates others by name and the nature of their offenses against Reason – the world's Dianne Feinsteins, Charles Schumers and Josh Sugarmanns – who between them have spun more fairy tales than the Brothers Grimm.

Thomas Paine wrote in his famous *Common Sense,* the tract that fundamentally informed the American Revolution:

> *I offer nothing more than simple facts, plain arguments, and common sense; and have no other preliminaries to settle with the reader, than that he will divest himself of prejudice and prepossession, and suffer his reason and his feelings to determine for themselves; that he will put on, or rather that he will not put off, the true character of a man, and generously enlarge his views beyond the present day.*

This proved a powerful invocation to critical thought. To say these were influential words is a great understatement. These words apply equally well to Guy Smith and *Shooting the Bull.*

Brian Anse Patrick
Associate Professor
University of Toledo
Author, *Rise of the Anti-Media*

# Chapter 1: The Guns That Never Were
(how Dianne Feinsteins lie)

Attempted homicide on a room full of reporters will, without question, scare them to the point of impromptu BVD changes.

Senator Dianne Feinstein, the vertically abbreviated representative from the formerly great state of California, did just that in what may be the single most effective political stunt in American history. While campaigning to preserve her 1994 ban on certain firearms, she created in the minds of freshly soiled journalists a sense of trauma that only comes from the near-death experience of staring down the business end of a high caliber rifle.

While preaching the demerits of so-called "assault weapons," Dianne Feinstein (known to friends and supporters as *Di Fi* and to political enemies as *Die Finally*) hoisted an AK-47 rifle to her hip, and with her finger on the trigger, swept its muzzle across the crowded room like a storm trooper clearing a Berlin ghetto. Audible gasps escaped from even battle-hardened yet suddenly sober reporters who, despite their chronic ignorance concerning firearms, understood two things with perfect clarity: first, it is never a good idea to be at the exit end of a rifle's barrel; second, Senator Feinstein was a lunatic with a gun.

Though pro-gun bloggers and assorted pundits dismissed this episode as gross stupidity on the part of the Careless California Caliph, the moment was in fact a staggeringly well-scripted act in an ongoing piece of political theater. Rabble cannot be roused to action without a sense of urgency, something that armed assault achieves with amazing rapidity. The AK-47 in her hands was Feinstein's Frankenstein, poised threateningly at the assembled post-modern town criers. With few exceptions, those reporters later bled pungent prose about the rampant danger of "assault weapons" in the hands of erratic criminals since they had personally faced that dual threat mere moments before.

Feinstein's stunt is our first lesson in that vein of political skullduggery known as "the art of lying." Indeed, hers was the type of lie from which most other policy lies – and most gun control lies in particular – flow. This fundament of all falsehood is effective mainly because it taps into responses dwelling beneath logic, reason and stained under britches.

> **The Lie of Fear:** Creating a false sense of fear in order to motivate people to action while easing them past critical thinking.

Fear drives all animals, including the untamed voter. Thus, fear drives most political action. Sarah Brady instills irrational fear of wanton carnage into the minds of pliable voters, and by their proxy enacts irrational firearm regulations. Second Amendment organizations instill rational fear of firearm confiscation into the minds of their members to defeat these same laws. Fear is, and always will be, *the* primal motivator and the tool of choice among politicos and propagandists. In this respect there is not a dime's worth of difference between Dianne Feinstein and Michael Moore. Well, that and several metric tons of undulating blubber.

Despite their angst-based agenda and unsavory methodologies, we can understand why both Dianne Feinstein and Sarah Brady hold fear in their own hearts and broadcast it at every opportunity to an anxious populace. Unlike nearly every other citizen of the United States, both Brady and Feinstein have endured harsh encounters with psychotic misuse of firearms, which resulted in psychotic misuse of Sarah and Dianne's influence and power.

It was the Monday after Thanksgiving in 1978, which in San Francisco is our summertime (others call it our annual *Indian Summer*, but in the politically correct intellectual gulag that is the Modern Sodom, such unsuitable language is *verboten*). On that otherwise beautiful day by the Bay, a former police officer and city supervisor named Dan White discovered, much to his dismay, that he would not be appointed to his former position of power by the mayor. Perhaps robbed of vital cranial blood flow from a Thanksgiving gorge, White bypassed building security at City Hall and shot the mayor along with another city supervisor.

On that day, Dianne Feinstein was president of San Francisco's Board of Supervisors. The City Hall shooting created new tasks and opportunities for this budding career politician that she seized upon with a gluttony only observed at all-you-can-eat buffets and campaign fundraising events: Feinstein automatically ascended to the Mayor's throne and was obligated to announce White's homicides to the media. This recombinant stew of instant power, media attention and a ready-made issue gave Feinstein the necessary tools to become a one-woman propaganda factory – one that has operated without interruption for nearly 30 years.

General Motors should achieve such a production record.

How the actions of one lone and inarguably insane policeman-turned-politician-turned-assassin should be the basis for restricting the privileges and immunities of an entire nation has yet to be reconciled outside of Feinstein's alleged mind. Personal acquaintance with a shooting victim seems to be a common motivator for such indiscriminate action. As it was with Senator Feinstein, so it was with Sarah Brady. Trauma apparently breeds a truth deficit disorder.

Less than three years after Dan White thinned the herd of politicians in San Francisco, a drifter named John Hinckley completed a journey by bus from Hollywood to Washington D.C., a pair of terminating points that have bizarre behavior as their uniting bond. A delusional and unilateral love affair with actress Jodie Foster caused Hinckley to attempt a unique variation of the old *impressing a girl* tactic, and using a gun he purchased six months prior, Hinckley attempted to ventilate President Ronald Reagan. As all presidents do, Reagan had in tow an entourage that caught several of Hinckley's stray bullets, thereby creating collateral damage including then presidential press secretary James Brady, husband of Sarah. The media, in their perpetual frenzy to report anything titillating and blood stained, reported to a stunned nation and to a stunned Brady family that James Brady had died.

Press rumors of Jim Brady's death were more than 29 years premature.

Nobody can blame Sarah Brady, and to a much lesser degree Dianne Feinstein, for feeling a bit traumatized. Yet individually these women fermented their personal distress into an intoxicant capable of inducing the political equivalent of beer goggles. Dianne and Sarah externalized their fear, feeling compelled to make everyone else share their dread, regardless of rational thought or the moral price paid by exercising the Lie of Fear. They were scared of death and intended to scare everyone to death so they would have neurotic company.

Instilling fear in other people requires a gimmick, which can be problematic. Dianne Feinstein can mock journalist genocide, but that gambit has a short shelf life and cannot be repeated without the ruse being revealed. Fear needs a face and a name that can be instantly personified and mindlessly parroted for maximum effect. Over the decades, the gun control industry has created numerous scarecrows with which to frighten magpie voters. Gun control groups invented the racist term "Saturday Night Special" to demonize inexpensive handguns. They renamed self-defense legislation as "shoot first laws" to paint portraits of the Wild West's resurrection. They went as far as to invent entire classifications of firearms that had never existed, causing the sales staff at Smith and Wesson to collectively swoon thinking they had somehow missed a market niche.

The gun control lobby invented "assault weapons" out of something thinner than air. What Jews are to Hitler and Ahmadinejad, assault weapons are to Dianne Feinstein, with the primary difference being that Jews actually exist.

**The Lie of Definition:** Using purposefully vague or misleading definitions to create political or legislative leverage, especially when it splits the opposing faction.

The Lie of Definition is of tactical and strategic importance in generating political power, where both the tactics and strategy depend on the definition being suitably imprecise. Tactically speaking, a sufficiently indistinct topic cannot be rapidly scrutinized. Vague definitions move speedily through the political ether without the resistance of review. This embeds the associated concept into the average human mind since the average human has insufficient time and resources to deeply investigate the topic. It also eases a complex subject under journalistic radar given constant pressures for meeting deadlines and the inconvenience of performing fact-checking during happy hour. Ask any political reporter for a local paper what the definition of an "assault weapon" is, and a cogent answer will not emerge, even if the reporter first passes a breathalyzer test.

The Lie of Definition has strategic political value as well. Properly written legislation has the disadvantage of clearly defining what is legal and what is not, which hinders misuse of the law. Many laws are written with an intentional lack of clarity to give law enforcement and the courts ample leeway in extracting punishment based on their biases. Vague laws allow your teenager to get a wrist slap for a youthful indiscretion but they have also allowed public lynching to go unchecked. Lawmakers and laws are not vague via idiocy (well, not all of the time) – they are vague for the specific purpose of being flexible to your disadvantage.

The more insidious strategic intent behind the Lie of Definition is that the very definition can be changed at will and after the fact. Therein lay the beauty of the manufactured phrase "assault weapon." An assault weapon became whatever a politician wanted it to be, and every assault weapon ban proposed or enacted was different from all the others. If "assault weapons" as a class of firearms actually existed, then banning such firearms would have the undesirable effect of limiting what Feinstein and fellow politicians could ban. Vagueness of classification allowed radically different prohibitions to be launched and to be expanded when convenient by either new legislation, or worse yet by bureaucratic edict – confiscation without representation if you will.

The Legal Community Against Violence, a well-funded band of political reprobates whose nefarious activities are legendary, demonstrated this plainly enough as they crusaded to salvage Feinstein's Federal assault weapons ban.

In their propaganda, the Legal Community Against Violence provide a frank confession to the Lie of Definition. Across eight jurisdictions, we find anywhere from 19 to 75 banned firearms, six differing generic classification schemes and several legal systems for banning more firearms without specific legislative action. This raft of contrary commandments might well have been created with random tosses of darts at the corner bar near the newspaper offices. You would be hard pressed to find any commonality among these laws or the firearms they banned.

Except that all those guns were ugly.

| Jurisdiction | Banned weapon types, models and series | Generic assault weapon features | Other weapons |
|---|---|---|---|
| Federal | 19 assault weapon types, models and series are named | Firearms w/ any 2 features and can accept a detachable magazine (latter does not apply to shotguns) | |
| California | 75 assault weapon types, models and series are named | Rifles and pistols: any 1 feature and can accept a detachable magazine. Shotguns: 2 features, or can accept a detachable magazine or revolving cylinder | CA Attorney General may petition court to add to the list of prohibited weapons |
| Connecticut | 67 assault weapon types, models and series are named | Uses federal definition | Conversion kits prohibited |
| Hawaii | | Uses federal definition – pistols only | |
| Maryland | 17 "assault pistol" types, models and series are named | | 66 assault weapon types, models and series are named and regulated but not banned |
| Massachusetts | 19 assault weapon types, models and series are named | Uses federal definition | "Large capacity weapons" are regulated but not banned |
| New Jersey | 63 assault weapon types, models and series are named | Fixed magazine rifles: >15 rounds. Shotguns: any 1 feature. Pistols: no generic feature definition | Conversion kits prohibited |
| New York | 19 assault weapon types, models and series are named | Uses federal definition | |

Table 1: Various assault weapon bans as listed in the LCAV's 2004 *Banning Assault Weapons – A Legal Primer for State and Local Action*.

## The Lie of Intimidation: Triggering instinctive reactions to create unfounded fears.

The only commonality these firearms generally had was that they were modeled after military machinery. They were not military weapons. There were no machine guns on the list. They were not combat ready. They could not spray rooms with bullets. They could do no more damage than a hunting rifle. Dianne Feinstein could not have wounded more than a couple of fleeing reporters with a common "assault weapon."

But they sure looked mean. Most were black with abbreviated stocks and short barrels. The rifles looked familiar to anyone who owned a television in the 20th century and watched war footage from Vietnam and Iraq. They looked like the M-16s our soldiers carried around the world. They looked like the MP5s British counter-terrorism forces toted at airports. They appeared identical to AK-47s carried by Al Qaeda insurgents and portly California senators. They were instantly intimidating to the uneducated masses who didn't hunt, who never served in the military, and were unable to tell the difference between a carbine and a carburetor.

This was precisely Josh Sugarmann's scheme. Sugarmann heads the Violence Policy Center (VPC), an organization that never met a gun control law over which it did not wet its nonprofit pants. In 1988, the VPC invented the new "assault weapon" agenda because their old agenda was not working. In their publication "Assault Weapons and Accessories in America," Sugarmann and crew bemoaned their continuing failure to encourage Mister and Missus America to hammer their Colt Pythons into plowshares. Sugarmann bluntly told his minions "… the issue of handgun restriction consistently remains a non-issue with the vast majority of legislators, the press and public." You have to give the boy credit for at least recognizing a lost cause when it kicks him in the political crotch.

Mounting failures for the gun control movement led Sugarmann to the stunning conclusion that he had not yet scared the public witless. In the incremental battle of disarmament, Sugarmann correctly identified a new strategy, one based on exploiting the relative ignorance of the public against them.

> "Assault weapons ... are a new topic. The weapons' menacing looks, *coupled with the public's confusion over fully automatic machine guns versus semi-automatic assault weapons* – anything that looks like a machine gun *is assumed to be a machine gun* – can only increase the chance of public support for restrictions on these weapons." (emphasis clearly mine)

The Lie of Intimidation is based on primal reactions. It only works if the audience holds associative images that trigger a gut-level response. Mention the phrase "sex with children" to anyone outside of NAMBLA or the priesthood, and they recoil in disgust. Show them a firearm that looks like, but is not, a military rifle and they will flinch at their mental video montage assembled from decades of televised war footage. They naturally associate the visual image of a look-alike firearm with the death and devastation of war and senatorial press conferences.

In the same way that flirting opens the heart and other vital organs to the romantic process, so is jabbing a military-looking firearm up the noses of reporters the initiation of a gun control movement. Once fear is established in the heart, the head becomes conveniently empty and ready to receive associated misinformation. Such scare tactics – the Lies of Fear and Intimidation – were sultry make-up and short skirts worn to open the hearts and fog the minds of voters concerning ugly guns. Dianne Feinstein and her cohorts in con, painted like shipyard hookers during Fleet Week, had their misinformation ready and waiting.

Nobody rushes to telephone their representative to enact bans on bunny rabbits and butterflies, and if they do we have facilities in which to treat their dementia, including Capitol Hill and the Palace of Westminster (though those institutions are reserved for the exceptional lunatics). Nor is it sufficient to be frightened by the momentary sight of a Fuzzy Lop or a Swallowtail. Mass fear, like mass religion, requires both indoctrinated dread and scripture that can be repeated rapidly, often and authoritatively regardless of any inconvenient reality. In short, there must be panic driven by mob psychology.

So what, precisely, was Dianne Feinstein so terrified of in 1994 when she first intimidated voters from coast to coast? Not much, it appears.

Taking some of the more expansive definitions for "assault weapon" we see that in 1993, the year before Feinstein's legislation was enacted, fewer than 1% of homicides were committed using these nebulous "assault weapons," though this number is over-estimated due to the source of the data. According to various state-level records, the rate was closer to 0.2%. There were approximately 18,000 firearm homicides in the United States that year. So in 1994, while Feinstein was intentionally inciting mass panic in the press population, the maximum homicide count from so-called "assault weapons" bordered on 36 deaths. That's not even a slow afternoon at a Chicago Democrat Pep Rally.

One problem with the Lies of Fear and Intimidation is that a little raw data can quickly destroy either. If Feinstein and Friends had relied only on homicide statistics, their argument would have evaporated the instant a bored cub reporter had a spare moment to call a cop and ask how many ugly guns they confiscated each month. People peddling Lies of Fear and Intimidation must come well armed with enough material to keep the average voter from investigating too deeply. There are many tactics for accomplishing this, but the most effective maneuver is making the problem appear multi-faceted, which brings us to Criminals, Cops and Conversions – an unholy trinity of untruth.

"Assault weapons" look menacing. An unshaven, tattooed street thug wielding an ugly gun is menace squared. It was natural that gun control organizations would attempt to tie the existence of mythical assault weapons with street-level slaughter caused by the common criminal. They had to convince the suburban American public that banning such firearms was, in effect, crime control. "Ban the ugly guns," so the story went, "and you ban the ugly criminals."

One does not have to go far to find evidence of this assault on sensibility. It is as close as Dianne Feinstein's web site, on a sadly lingering page titled "Assault Weapons Support" where there exists a rotating graphic of full-sized rifles – M-16s, AK-47s and assorted long guns, uniformly painted black – with the captioned claim "These guns are often used [by] criminals going into a major criminal event – who are seeking to do the maximum damage possible in the shortest amount of time." Feinstein personally confirms the criminal/carbine connection.

But this doesn't jibe with criminological data or basic physics.

Criminals require a certain element of surprise to be good at their jobs. They are fond of concealing their often stolen guns on their often doped bodies since that is the one place where their weaponry will always be with them – readily available and portable to the scene of their crimes. Since a stubby AK-47 measures in at 870 millimeters, and the average male torso is a mere 600 vertical millimeters, hiding an "assault weapon" on their person is a challenge, even when wearing large and puffy parkas during the dog days of summer, which is in vogue among modern gangsters. The situation gets worse when an unfortunate hoodlum cannot find an abbreviated AK, and must jam a full length M-16 (1,006mm) under his arm, presumably with the muzzle jutting past his cheek and lifting his sweat jacket hood a few inches into the air like a cranial pup tent.

We cannot expect Senator Feinstein to master basic mathematics, but asking law enforcement about criminal use of ugly guns is certainly the minimal research that she or her staff or her interns – in either her cozy Washington D.C. office or any of her four California headquarters – should have committed. Assuredly, the local constabulary would have relevant information concerning the criminal misuse of so-called "assault weapons." Police would certainly be vocal on the matter if they stared down the barrels of "assault weapons" as often as journalists covering senatorial press conferences.

This is precisely why Dianne didn't investigate. Asking law enforcement for facts or perspective would have violated the first rule of political mythmaking and Maier's Law of Research: If the facts do not conform to the theory, the facts must be disposed of.

"Assault rifles have never been an issue in law enforcement," opined Joseph Constance, the Deputy Chief of Police in Trenton, NJ while testifying before the Senate Judiciary Committee in August 1993, the year before Feinstein railroaded her "assault weapon" ban through Congress and forwarded it to the eagerly awaiting Prince of Photo Ops, Bill Clinton. "I have been on this job for 25 years and I haven't seen a drug dealer carry one. They are not used in crimes, they are not used against police officers." No wonder Feinstein started toting AK-47s around Capitol Hill – she was prepared to shoot cops who might talk to reporters.

"Since police started keeping statistics," he continues, "we now know that assault weapons are/were used in an underwhelming 0.026 of 1% of crimes in New Jersey. This means that my officers are more likely to confront an escaped tiger from the local zoo than to confront an assault rifle in the hands of a drug-crazed killer on the streets."

Yet Dianne Feinstein could not be bothered to write a law banning escaped tigers. Indeed a law against escaped tigers would be as effective as most any gun control law, because tigers and criminals obey only one law, that being of the jungle.

Constable Constance was on target about criminals having little use for assault weapons. The Federal Bureau of Investigations started maintaining a uniform database of crime statistics before Feinstein could spell "slush fund." Criminologists nationwide dove into the publicly available numbers while the "assault weapon" ban debate raged. Simple math showed that an American was eleven times *more* likely to be beaten to death than to be killed with the fictitious "assault weapons." Since most homicides are side effects from other criminal activity, there was a clear non-relationship between criminals and ugly guns. This reality threatened the "ugly gun" = "ugly criminal" connection, chiseling dangerously away at the foundation of Feinstein's fraud.

Police opinions were validated by the *New England Journal of Medicine* which dug through the details of 583 drive-by shootings in Los Angeles three years prior to the Federal assault weapon ban. In dirty old L.A., which is submerged in gangland drug violence, only one incident appeared to involve an assault weapon. Criminologists echoed similar conclusions in the *Journal of California Law Enforcement* by reporting, "It is interesting to note, in the current hysteria over semi-automatic and military look-alike weapons, that the most common weapon used to murder police officers was that of the .38 Special and the .357 Magnum revolver." Even Sarah Brady has yet to classify a .38 caliber revolver as an assault weapon, though it is on next year's project list.

This disruption of illusion did not stop the gun control industry's myth machine from manufacturing more fraud. We honor our police for many solid reasons, the foremost being that they voluntarily allow themselves to be endangered by criminals (you know, the people *not* using assault weapons) and keep us from having to do so ourselves. We value our cops almost as much as we value our children and go out of our way to protect them, except in Los Angeles where it is every man and cop for himself. Since Feinstein needed backup ammunition to protect her proposed ban, she positioned police as a shield between facts and her proposed legislation. Soon the airwaves were dripping with claims that many police officers were killed with "assault weapons" while on duty. Papers recycled the claim like yesterday's newsprint, and Feinstein's cop-friendly yet fraudulent assertion went largely unchallenged by hung-over Fourth Estate fact checkers.

Sadly, cops do get shot. And aside from suicides, they are most often shot by the thugs from whom they protect us. According to the National Law Enforcement Officers Memorial Fund, over time 36% of on-duty police deaths are from gunshots (for perspective's sake, 29% of police duty deaths are from automobile accidents). We owe these brave servants of the people more gratitude than they ever receive for simply being in the line of fire. Those who fall deserve more than we can ever give.

Yet "assault weapons" are barely on the list of worries for cops, and are so far from the top of that list as to be lost in statistical noise. If cops encountered "assault weapon" armed thugs as often as civilians do, then approximately 0.36% of dead police officers would have been killed with ugly guns. Criminologists who were patient enough to drill through detailed reports tallied about a 1% rate. Yet HCI (Handgun Control, Inc., the name of Sarah Brady's organization before she became the gun control industry's figurehead) claimed that 13% of police officers killed were shot with "assault weapons." There is a staggering gulf between the two numbers, with Sarah's estimates being 36 times what the FBI considered rational. How could the FBI and Sarah Brady's team be so far apart, especially considering that HCI used FBI data as their raw material for manufacturing their myths? Not even Amelia Earhart missed by that margin.

This is where the Lie of Definition comes into play. Models of firearms that were not previously contemplated as assault weapons were magically included in Sarah's list when the need to protect cops arose. Indeed, the number of cops killed by "assault weapons" spanned such a wide range that gun control groups either used different definitions for "assault weapons," studied different countries, or pulled the numbers directly out of their southern-most orifice. This unseemly variation on the rabbit-in-the-hat trick continued into the next century when Feinstein's assault weapon ban was scheduled to evaporate unless its usefulness could be proven. One year before the sun set on this part of the gun control empire, the Violence Policy Center – an organization that openly advocates banning all handguns – claimed that one in five police officers were killed with assault weapons. This is a curious conclusion concerning the effectiveness of Feinstein's decade-long ban. The VPC claimed that 20% of cops were killed by firearms that had been banned for ten years after Brady's HCI claimed a 13% rate before the ban. If these numbers could be believed (which they couldn't) then the situation for our brave men and women in blue got worse after Feinstein enacted her ban. Dianne apparently had endangered cops as thoroughly as she had reporters.

Liars display a curiously common trait. When cornered, their assertions become more tangent. Like a magician whose left hand distracts your attention away from what his right hand is doing, so did the gun control industry when the functional equivalency between "assault weapons" and hunting rifles was made. The fact is that the ugly guns Dianne Feinstein banned fired at the same rate and fired the same bullets as those used by hunters worldwide, especially hog hunters down south who prefer the light weight and durability of "assault weapons" when slogging through swamps. Functionally speaking, Feinstein's "assault weapons" were no more menacing that what your Uncle Bob used to bag the boar whose head hangs over the mantle. An honest gun-banning lobby cannot invoke fear in the general population when their symbol of evil is no more wicked than Cousin Ralph's tin can plinking toy.

The gun control industry is, if nothing else, resourceful. Feinstein, Sugarmann and Brady parried, founding new fear factors by making "assault weapons" what they are not.

The common civilian image of military weapons is those that fire a steady stream of bullets. We have grown accustomed to such scenes from all manner of war movies or watching warfare on the evening news. Since the firearms Feinstein wanted to ban were visually similar to big- and small-screen footage of military weaponry, it was a convenient distraction to claim that these ugly guns could be readily converted to full military capabilities – turned into machine guns. Images of hardened criminals hammering Uncle Bob's hunting rifle into spray fire, grenade-launching weapons of mass destruction were crafted for a bloodthirsty media.

The only WMDs present were Witless Mass Delusions.

Ignore for a moment that it was already illegal to sell firearms that could be "readily converted" into machine guns. Nothing on Feinstein's list of banned sports rifles can be readily converted according to the Bureau of Alcohol, Tobacco, Firearms and Explosives, the agency charged with policing firearms in America, and who from their title also appear to be in charge of regulating entertainment in Detroit. Long-standing legislation from the dry days of Prohibition prevented such firearms from being made, distributed, sold or converted. In effect, Feinstein was attempting to ban something that did not exist, or at least should not exist if the Federal government was doing its assigned job. This was a complex calumny beyond the expertise or patience of the average voter, standard-issue reporters and apparently a slate of seemingly sober elected officials (which, by his gin-blossom expression, excludes John McCain).

Yet, a more basic question should have come to the collective minds of all interested observers: If these ugly guns could be easily converted into full-auto, rock-and-roll death machines, why weren't they? Surely if these firearms could be easily converted, and if criminals were as fond of them as Feinstein feigned, there would be daily high-caliber death matches on most every street corner in the United States and cops would be dropping faster than pants at a Barney Frank pool party.

Americans remained vertical and strolling the streets because nobody was converting these ugly guns, whether due to the complexity of the process, a relative lack of criminal usefulness for heavy firepower, or existing laws against peddling convertible armament. Jimmy Trahin, a detective in the criminal paradise called Los Angeles – part of Feinstein's turf – told the Committee on the Judiciary, Subcommittee on the Constitution that a mere 0.15% of over 4,000 weapons confiscated in Los Angeles in one year were converted for full-auto firepower, and that only 0.3% of these guns had any evidence of an attempt to convert. Simply put, thugs were either not interested in upgrading armament or they were too stupid for any other line of work outside of the Beltway.

We must then marvel at the attempt and at the temporary success achieved by this cabal of canard casters. Together, Dianne Feinstein, the Violence Policy Center, the Legal Community Against Violence and Sarah Brady's own Handgun Control, Inc. invented a term for firearms that never existed. They varied the definition to suit local political expediencies. They painted a horrific portrait of criminal mobs happily adapting hunting rifles to machines of massacre aimed menacingly at the blue line that separates you from the violence of the felonious fraternity. By the tiniest of margins (two votes in the House of Representatives) Feinstein's assault weapon ban passed and a non-problem became the centerpiece for many supporting politicians, who were summarily voted out of office in the next election cycle.

Given that these so-called "assault weapons" were barely a blip on the criminological radar, why did so many people work so hard, lie so thoroughly and risk their political futures to have Feinstein's assault weapon ban passed? They did so for reasons well beyond just "assault weapons." Their end goals lay beyond eliminating a tiny number of ugly guns from the market. They worked hard to achieve just one goal, and one goal only. Charles Krauthammer summarized Sarah's end game when he wrote in the *Washington Post*:

> "Passing a law like the assault weapons ban is
> a symbolic, purely symbolic move ... Its only real
> justification is not to reduce crime but to desensi-

tize the public to the regulation of weapons in preparation for their ultimate confiscation."

As we will soon see, this end game has grown beyond a few military look-alikes, and now engulfs all firearms, all countries and the United Nations. You have to lie big to fool an entire planet.

# Chapter 2: The Carnage That Never Occurred
## (how Josh Sugarmanns lie)

My friends want me to leave California so they can carry guns in public.

I lived in Florida most of my life, leaving in 1988, the year after the land of snakes, gators and pterodactyl-size mosquitoes passed legislation allowing any adult devoid of a criminal record to carry a loaded firearm in public, providing it was tucked away under a coat or in a handbag. After fleeing Florida, I lived in Virginia, a state happily lacking in alligators, but one that passed Concealed Carry of Weapons (CCW) legislation in 1995, a year before I headed to the Leftist Coast. It seems whenever I leave a state, that state grants citizens the legal right to pack heat. Thus, my gunny pals here in San Francisco are offering me a one-way ticket to any other state, nation or planet.

In medieval ages (circa 1988), only ten states allowed citizens to tote protection. One of those states did not "allow" concealed carry per se. They simply never bothered to pass any laws against it, believing in the quaint and libertarian notion that not dying at the hands of marauding criminals was a civil right. So when a vertically challenged, middle-aged woman in the form of Marion Hammer decided to bring similar legal latitude to Floridians, I had a front-row seat on the opening salvo of the greatest of gun control wars, and a full view of intellectual carnage at the intersection of free speech and political tarradiddle.

When Florida's concealed carry legislation was first proposed, gun control advocacy groups were apoplectic with indignation. The very idea that legislation should make it easier for people to use guns defied every fib the gun control industry had told themselves for years (given repeated legislative failures, these organizations appeared to be the only ones still sniffing their own fetor). Worse yet, the liberalizing legislation was being proffered by a *woman*! The very notion that a member of that group – a pack supposedly swayed by the gun control industry's Lies of Fear and Intimidation – would defy Sarah Brady and Dianne Feinstein, much less take their political football the wrong way down the field, was enough to give Pete Shields the shingles (Shields, the chairman emeritus of Handgun Control, which later morphed into Sarah Brady's battalion, once advised the public that when confronted by violent criminals they should "put up no defense — give them what they want, or run").

Thus began the Florida concealed carry debate, though "debate" affords the process far too much dignity. Lobbyists from Handgun Control, VPC and similarly suspect organizations descended I-95 from their comfy Washington, D.C. nests, creating a rancor heretofore unknown outside of war zones and Berkeley drum circles. Opponents of Marion Hammer's concealed carry proposal universally shared two rhetorical traits: They were loud and they were hysterical.

Being boisterous and boorish has, unfortunately, become the norm for political discourse in the United States. There remain only a few who can trade barbed retorts with enough civility to still be considered sober. Out-shouting opponents has become the tactic of choice for those who have opinions and lack supporting data. In 1987 Florida, the problem gun control groups faced was that criminological data was not favorable to banning concealed carry, much less to banning guns in general. For the first time since the passage of the Gun Control act of 1968, the gun control industry was on the defensive, leaving them few tactics aside from ratcheting-up fear, intimidation, tumult and decibels.

Before little Marion Hammer ignited the Florida firestorm, concealed carry was available to citizens in small states like New Hampshire, or uninhabitable ones like North Dakota. People are different in small-population states, which is to say they are not normal, and by "not normal" I mean they are civil. In small-population states, either everyone knows everyone else, or they live so far apart that they commune only at school and church. Either extreme leads to situations where felons find few opportunities for criminal mischief. The few that do are incarcerated or killed during the act, and thus crime rates in these states coast well under national averages.

The problem faced by the flock of gun control lobbyists – who in 1987 migrated to Florida like retired Yankees – was that the existing crime data did not paint the right picture, namely a portrait dripping in blood. If Pete Shields and Josh Sugarmann had pointed to North Dakota and proclaimed, "Look at that violent cesspool of gun-toting inhumanity!" the good folks in Florida would have provided Pete and Josh a pair of tightly tailored jackets, with extra long sleeves that could be wrapped around the back and buckled (which still might not be a bad idea for Sugarmann). Data showed an underwhelming amount of gun-based violent crime occurring in pistol-packing provinces. FBI databases informed everyone that the odds of being a victim of violent crime were roughly 31 times higher in the sophisticated and nearly "gun-free" metropolis of New York than in beautiful downtown Bismarck. It is hard to instill fear in the minds of the masses by vilifying a state where the prevailing cause of death is terminal boredom.

**The Lie of Omission:** Purposefully excluding information to inappropriately change beliefs about an issue.

The Lie of Omission is the quintessential political arabesque. Novelist Robert Heinlein noted that of the two best ways to lie, one was to tell the truth but to omit a critical fact. By misplacing key details, any catastrophe can be remade into a success or vice versa. If gun control advocates had supplied Florida voters with all relevant information about concealed carry in other states, gun control would have achieved as much traction as a Texan driving in an ice storm, and with the same terminal results. Nobody from the gun control lobby spoke of Indiana, New Hampshire, South Dakota or Vermont. Doing so would have been political hari-kari (which, incidentally, is performed with a dagger and not a firearm).

Gun control propaganda was not helped by the fact that tiny ladies and law enforcement officers (LEOs) were backing packing. When the Florida Chiefs of Police Association and other law enforcement fraternities gave their blessing to the concealed carry legislation, the good people of Florida yawned. Even the media failed to gain consciousness and report the primary human interest story that was Marion Hammer – a pageboy-coifed gal standing five-foot-nothing, who was named the Roy Rogers 1985 "Man of the Year" (being the only woman ever to receive that award), and who was the public spokesperson for the proposal. Florida's legislature, more notorious for coddling entertainment empires than controversial gun control laws, was poised to pass the law with a margin wide enough to compensate for nominal bribery.

Florida's population was the gun control lobby's main problem. With almost thirteen million people busily shooting surplus alligators that routinely crawled into their back yards, gun control groups had to incite panic on a mammoth scale just to be heard. Mere fear would not do! The good people of Florida had to believe that they faced imminent death at the hands of every gun owner in the state, which in 1987 equaled the number of non-incarcerated adults plus most of their kids. Spurring mass hysteria was complicated by the fact that Floridians stared death in the face every morning, be it from ill-tempered hurricanes dancing cha chas across their homes, or the hit-and-run driving tactics of retirees encountering their first cerebral strokes while piloting Cadillacs through grocery store parking lots and over city sidewalks. It would take a lot to scare the average Floridian.

### The Lie of Looming Catastrophe: Using worst case scenarios, regardless of how remote, to instill a fear of uncontrollable danger.

They did their best. The redoubtable rhetoric of gun control advocates still rings in the ears of Sunshine State natives. HCI spoke of cataclysms putting in mortal danger every inebriated spring break coed and all the paste-white Disney World tourists. Newspaper editorialists came alarmingly close to portraying Mickey Mouse mowing down fields of small children in fits of rodent rage. The Sugarmanns and Shields of the gun control world made the Apocalypse look, by comparison, like a tickle fight. Some of the lissom lines lobbed by the fulminating gun control industry included:

"The gutters will run red ..."

"Expect shooting over fender bender accidents ..."

"You will be mistaken for someone else and shot in the street ..."

"When an angry parent starts shooting up your school after an argument at a PTA meeting ..."

"Florida will become the Gunshine state!"

Yes, they actually thought up stuff *that* hokey.

Fast-moving hyperbole became the norm from one side of the debate, and at deafening levels. Deception's speed and volume were well calculated. Mark Twain accurately noted, "A lie can travel halfway around the world while the truth is putting on its shoes." In the political warfare that surrounds pending legislation, lies and emotions have a great tactical advantage. Both constitute the fuel of political momentum – what folks in the marketing trades call "buzz." Marketers and politicos build buzz by making concepts quick to understand and easy to pass along. When gun control groups discovered they had no substantial or supporting facts, data or historical perspective, they knew they at least had the advantage of our 15-second attention span world. Tidy sound bites backed with sloppy information could be communicated instantly and invoke enough dread that some listeners would blindly pass it along. Telling such tales takes a few seconds, but debunking the lie takes much longer. Every time a professional political provocateur found a TV camera and said, "Gun fights in the streets of Tallahassee," law enforcement chiefs and pint-sized ladies would have to patiently explain why there were no shoot-outs up north in Concord and Montpelier. Panic comes in small, portable packages whereas truth doesn't even fit in the overhead bin.

Through this circus of deceit, two elements kept Floridians speculating about the sanity of carpet-bagging gun control lobbyists. First, Florida was not that far beyond its rural past. Only recently had air conditioning made the state livable by mortals. NASA had brought international brain power to Florida's coast a couple of decades earlier, and Disney had only twenty years of experience cycling tourists through Florida at a rate fast enough that a few of them got stuck there. Though Florida's population was growing rapidly, a mere twenty years earlier Orlando was known mainly for orange groves – for a high time, local residents went to bustling Kissimmee to attend the weekly livestock auction. As is typical for rural folk, most Florida residents owned guns, shot regularly, had rifle racks in their pick-up trucks, and could not for the life of them understand all the fuss raised by an infestation of gun control campaigners.

Glove compartments were also an issue. Until the late 1980s, Florida law was vague about if and when one could carry a firearm in their vehicle. Case law wasn't entirely helpful, leaving a prevailing belief among law enforcement and citizens that anyone could carry a firearm in their glove compartment providing the door was closed. Some court rulings led to the informal "three distinct movements" rule, which said that you were allowed to carry a firearm in your vehicle if it took three or more distinct movements before you could fire (open glove compartment, grab gun, and remove it from the holster – or if you played fast and loose with the law, the final move was to disengage the safety). To say that carrying a handgun in the glove compartment was occasionally practiced by Floridians is akin to saying Ted Kennedy occasionally drank. It was common for crackers to carry a handgun in the car, and thus it was a tiny philosophical step for most Floridians to consider carrying their pistols everywhere else.

But "most" is not "all." Gun control lobbyists realized that manipulating the minority was the only card left to play. In any crowd you will find one or more people prone to panic. This is why yelling "fire" in a crowded theater is considered uncouth, as it only takes one person's panic to start a stampede. In this, people are not all that different from cattle, and having worked both bovine and voters, I can attest to these and other unfortunate similarities. Raising an emotive riot was the gun control industry's one and only chance to overwhelm the otherwise sedate Florida populace – the same people who already kept spare handguns in their glove compartments.

Winning was an imperative for the gun control lobby. Florida was no longer a backwater state. Though concealed carry laws had passed recently in Indiana, Maine and the Dakotas, Florida had enough size, population and large metropolitan areas to break the existing rural/urban divide on gun control. In 1987 there was a distinct delineation between large cities and the rest of the country, which persists to this day (view any county-by-county presidential election map from any recent election and you will see how intellectually isolated the big cities have become). So too, it is with gun control. There was great danger to the anti-gun apparatchik in losing a concealed carry fight in the newly bustling republic of Florida. They knew that if Florida passed concealed carry legislation, and open warfare did not erupt on the streets, then other large states might follow Florida's lead. The gun control industry had to preserve self-aggrandizing cerebral sanctity for bastions of civility like Chicago and New York City. If gun control proponents lost their ability to make city folk look down their collective noses at "the hicks," even large and liberal states could eventually fall and gun control as a movement would lose its base, momentum, money and power.

Which is exactly what happened.

In 1987, rhetoric poured onto Florida streets in the same way that blood didn't. Nary a day passed that an editor, especially those running scandal rags in larger towns, did not prophesy a humid holocaust in the swelter state. These alleged journalists would often invent their own predictions, crafting lurid tales of the street corner carnage to come. Others reprinted the accusations provided by HCI without the burdens of research or critical thinking. TV stations ran logically disconnected "human interest" stories about some poor slob who was gunned down, though a little digging typically showed that the assailant – and often the victim – were ex-cons with rap sheets longer than a Bill Clinton alibi.

### The Lie of Association: Using invalid associations to demonize a person or position.

The Lie of Association is a bedrock of the gun control industry. Average people have a fairly clear concept of good and bad, and thus have a fairly clear view of good and bad people. Left unmolested, the standard-issue voter is capable of rationally discriminating between the neighbor who has a handgun in his glove compartment, and the career criminal with violent tendencies and a record to prove it. One would hope gun control organizations might make the same distinction, but doing so kicks the legs out from under half of their position statements. By failing to make these distinctions, Josh Sugarmann and Pete Shields cast your Uncle Jim, your war buddy Dave and you as murderous thugs prone to wild rampages of homicidal indiscretion. Amalgamating society's good and the evil is an obtuse variation of "moral equivalency," with the obscene side effects of diminishing the sins of criminals while casting aspersions upon the average Joe. Clearly such comparisons are invalid, as would be a comparison that cast all singers as lunatics based solely on artistic association with Barbra Streisand.

Florida's legislature passed the concealed carry law, only to be vetoed by then governor and perpetual odd job Bob Graham. Yet Floridians, who have gamely survived the worst that Mother Nature can muster, kept passing the law again and again until a new governor replaced the defective one and concealed carry legislation became law. Gun control promoters filed the predictable lawsuits, but Floridians did what the firearm prohibitionists feared most: They lined up to get their concealed carry permits, forming queues longer than those at a Disney World E-ticket ride. The scramble for concealed carry certificates rivaled the Florida land rush of the 1920s, but with less loss of life and capital. The vote was in, the permits were out and the great experiment began.

And nothing happened.

Despite issuing more than 188,000 permits (nearly 2% of the adult population) in the first few years, there was an amazing lack of slaughter. Gun control lobbyists had insisted there would be homicides over automobile collisions, yet Florida's homicide rate fell from 36% above the national average to 4% below, before a nation-wide trend toward lower violent crime began. Other categories of violent crime didn't go down much if at all, but none went up either. Crime rates stayed steady or went lower, all while Florida's population density grew, the weather got hotter, hurricanes mauled the state and the

Dolphins started sinking. In fact, the only extra shootings that occurred were hunters attempting to bag enough alligators to make a decent pair of boots and a matching belt.

So what became of the bloodthirsty populace – the 200,000 folks who obtained the concealed carry paperwork and menaced the streets of Tampa, Miami and Chattahoochee? Some 350 licenses – 0.2% of those issued – were revoked. Of the tickets pulled from the public, 43% of them were for administrative issues (including a few people with criminal convictions – to whom the state was supposed to avoid issuing licenses). Forty-seven percent had them yanked after committing crimes not involving firearms, and a whopping 17 people had their licenses annulled for firearm violations, though not all of these were for violent crimes. It seems Florida can't even get a decent class of criminals, aside from the State Supreme Court.

Since Florida has wrested away from California the title of "Most Bizarre State in the Union," we might dismiss the lack of spontaneous concealed carry violence on the quaint nature of the region, its graying population or that it is just too damn hot to raise a loaded handgun at your neighbor. Despite serviceable demographics, this single experiment could not constitute a viable study of the claims made by gun control groups – that liberalized concealed carry laws would create a modern "Dodge City East." To make their case they needed other states with large populations and urban centers to demonstrate the catastrophe awaiting an armed society.

They rapidly got thirty one more.

After a short breather in which the people reevaluated their Florida vacation plans, freedom-focused activists started enacting concealed carry laws – modeled after Florida's – across the entire country. Like dominoes falling to gravity, significant states with significant political clout started issuing packing permits to pedestrians. The results resembled the predictions of the gun control industry in the same way that Rosie O'Donnell resembles a woman. Atlanta breathed a sigh of relief and her people returned to downtown for renewed night life. Volunteer State residents volunteered opinions on how lightweight Glocks felt tucked in their hip holsters. That den of evil and iniquity (no, no, not Washington, D.C.) Las Vegas allowed residents and even visitors from other compatible concealed carry states to pack pistols in purses. Even the citizens of Cleveland couldn't resist the appeal of not fearing criminals or gun control lobbyists.

Nor could the good people of Richmond, Virginia where I was parked for seven years. Unlike other metro regions bordering on a million denizens, Richmond in the mid 1990s was experiencing an odd crime wave, with homicides nearly doubling from the year when Florida passed its "shall issue" concealed carry law. Armed robberies and assaults were also gaining in popularity among the thuggery despite a one-handgun-a-month law enacted in 1993. Despite these new-found crimes being uniquely confined to drug dealers in housing projects, the average Richmondite was feeling none too secure for an evening at the Flood Zone or the Tobacco Factory. Richmond would have rather welcomed back General Grant than put up with petty street gangsters.

Virginia, being a little rural and collectively sane, thought that its concealed carry law should be updated, changing from a provincial system whereby the local constabulary might or might not issue a concealed carry permit as their whims so dictated, to a scheme modeled after Florida where anyone without an arrest record got paper. In most parts of Virginia not subservient to the massive gravity of state government (Richmond) or the Federal Government (D.C.), firearms were quite the norm. Neighbors knew their neighbors, and what few thugs existed outside of the ranks of career politicians were routinely shot, though shooting politicians out of pure moral principle was not beyond consideration. When proposals for a uniform "shall issue" concealed carry law erupted, familiar cries rose across the rolling Richmond hillsides:

"The gutters will run red …"

"Expect shooting over fender bender accidents …"

"You will be mistaken for someone else and shot in the street ..."

"When an angry parent starts shooting up your school after an argument at a PTA meeting ..."

"Virginia is for murderers!"

(Really guys, Madison Avenue is littered with copywriters whose worst television commercial prose is better than that. And they are cheap. Spend a buck and come up with some passable copy. After all, you only have nine states left in which to test new slogans.)

Aside from indefensible gun control industry predictions, there was another similarity to the great concealed carry debate in Florida – gun control activists did not mention how liberalized concealed carry was working in other states. In Virginia, gun controllers were silent on the Sunshine State. Activists avoided advertising Florida, for whom they had earlier issued the same frantic predictions, because doing so would have negated their resurrected rhetoric. In the few years between Florida passing its concealed carry and Virginia debating doing the same, Florida's population rose 14%, but its violent crime rate dropped 4%. Murders, the pestilence prophesied by pistol prohibitionists, plummeted 36%, and robberies largely fell into inactivity, declining 26%. The one thing HCI and VPC did not want to discuss was Florida. Like a three-card Monty dealer diverting your gaze, professional prohibitionists changed the subject whenever Alligator Alley was mentioned.

If you have never been to Virginia, you have missed meeting a unique society. The state is blessed with a matchless blend of intellectual acumen and down-home common sense. Virginians are too civil to say you are bulging with buncombe, yet they can spot it before it comes down from D.C. Southern gentility requires both a polite response to disingenuous carpetbaggers, and dismissing them from all future adult discussion. It did not take the average Virginian long to determine which of the two sides in the concealed carry debate were articulating their positions from their posteriors, and to develop a courteous condemnation thereof.

Pete Shields' clones thus recreated their first handicap, as they had in Florida, by not knowing the locals, their personalities and perceptions. It only got worse from there as the gun control industry faced every hurdle in Virginia that they faced in Florida, with the only relief being that Virginians had greater attention spans since they spent less time rescuing small children and family pets from gators. Virginia dwellers were predisposed to carrying firearms in their autos, were still largely and romantically influenced by their rural past, and they clearly understood the difference between friends and felons. If this were not bad enough news for Sarah Brady and her ilk, Virginians had the gumption to inquire about what had not happened in Florida and were not at all surprised by the results. When a rare Richmond liberal would fret over bumper car battles, the more common Old Dominion libertarian would ask, "Why isn't Jacksonville awash in blood?" If an Arlington avant-garde shrieked over suburban slayings, a refined Roanoke resident would retort, "Not seeing that in Pensacola." Gun control was suffering from a lack of gore in the Gunshine State.

As I slowly made the decision to head west, my fellow Virginians decided to allow any citizen without a rap sheet to pack heat. In the decade since my departure Virginia has endured Florida's fate – a shrinking violent crime rate despite a growing population. Since passing their concealed carry law in 1995, the population has gone up 13% but the state's violent crime rate dropped 24%. All the homicides that Richmond's regions suffered are abated by a state-wide drop in murders of 32%. And 13% fewer women have been raped.

And to this day the gun control groups are muttering, "What a lousy thing to happen to Virginia."

Human nature is predictable. One invariable is that people avoid things that can kill them with the exception of cigarettes, saturated fats, sex with strangers and bungee jumping. As all eyes turned to Florida and witnessed the conjectured carnage that was not, a new question was soon on the lips of gun owners everywhere: "Why not here?" The sound of that question uttered, amplified by upwards of 53% of households that owned one or more guns, got pretty loud and legislators across the purple mountains and fruited plains, fearing unemployment and succumbing to statistical evidence, copied Florida law. Like wagon train migrations, from east to west, Georgia and the Carolinas, Oklahoma and Arkansas, Texas and Wyoming all became right-to-carry states. By the summer of 2009, a full 41 of the 50 states allowed peaceful citizens to menace street thugs, and being capable of simple risk-reward analysis, the street thugs ran for cover.

Certainly, with four fifths of all states allowing concealed carry, the gun control industry should have had some real violence to demonstrate. Such a large-scale experiment would certainly show that across population densities, urban and rural conclaves and red-blue political divides, concealed carry laws would provoke enough random shootings to create a curve on the FBI's violence charts. In this mass of humanity exceeding 65% of the humanoids in the United States, opponents of concealed carry certainly had more than ample data to back their prognostications of obliteration and would be shouting the data from every rooftop, from Charleston to Chico.

If you hear crickets in the background, don't be surprised. The "Florida Experiment" became the "National Experiment," and like any well-designed experiment, the results are reproducible. Though the population grew nationally by about 21%, violent crime dropped 24%, homicides 34%, and rapes 14%. This drop sure wasn't due to a lack of handguns, the stockpile of which grew throughout the 1990s as people bought spares to tuck in belts or stuff in bras. In the 1990's we collectively enjoyed more freedom and an ongoing peep show at the White House. But we did not see the gutters run red with neighbors capping neighbors over loud stereos.

Except there was massive gun violence in a few select regions – where carrying a concealed firearm was verboten, and private ownership was illegal or legislatively discouraged. In the first decade after Florida kicked off the tidal wave of camouflaged cannons, violent crime crept up in Maryland (10%), trotted forward in Massachusetts (14%), leapt in D.C. (26%) and exploded in Delaware (82%). But of all these areas, Washington D.C., the cradle of liberty and the crib of political corruption, a city that made firearm ownership more criminal than child molesting and taking a bribe, boasted a homicide rate 57% higher while Florida's sank 39%. Yes, Washington D.C., beacon to the world's oppressed, with its own huddled masses yearning to keep breathing.

Two questions arise from the grand national experiment. First, did liberalized concealed carry laws passed throughout the 1990s and early 21st century help with the dropping crime rates everywhere outside of Dover and D.C.? Second, given the statistical dearth of death, would gun control groups quit echoing their well-rehearsed lies of omission, catastrophe and association? The first question is difficult to answer and beyond the patience of anyone not employed as a statistician or otherwise without a social life. The second question is very easy to answer – of course the gun control groups changed their messages. They now utilize forms of falsity so creative that even veteran politicos drop jaws in amazement.

Even while consumed by frigid San Francisco summer days, the coldest winds blow from the Brady Campaign and the Violence Policy Center web sites. Following each to special pages bursting with purple prose on the subject, we discover that the overwhelming popularity of, and completely carnage-free effects from liberalized carry laws have not changed Sarah Brady's or Josh Sugarmann's opinions. What they have done, instead, is to increase the level of misdirection.

**The Lie of Lewinsky:** Forcefully making flat denials of observable fact to cast doubt in otherwise lucid minds.

The Brady Campaign initiates inaccuracies by reporting that "carrying concealed weapons does not make America safer." The implicated falsehood at play here is that concealed carry makes America less safe. But as the FBI statistics testify, America is certainly not less safe, and is arguably more peaceful. Yet Sarah's staff writers avoid offering anything that resembles evidence like they (or you for that matter) can find at the Bureau of Justice Statistics web site – an online database of state- and national-level crime trend estimates, drawn from the FBI Uniform Crime Statistics.

Perhaps Sarah finds numbers confusing.

"Do You Feel Safer Sitting Next to Someone Carrying a Gun?" Actually, yes, I do. When visiting Reno, Nevada a few years back I shared a diner booth with some old friends, and a new one. The new fellow at the table was a lifelong Reno resident and he had a discernable forty-five caliber bulge beneath his jacket. At that diner, in that town so notorious for gambling and divorce, I felt safer than I would on any evening stroll I might take in Chicago or Newark. Given that 65% of the citizens in the United States may well be sitting beside someone with a concealed firearm every day, that they voted for this situation, and that their violent crime rates have fallen everywhere they voted these laws in, I suspect they feel safer too.

Sarah's statements devolve from the abject to the absurd in rapid fashion: "… in April 1999, Missouri citizens voted against liberalizing that state's CCW laws in the first-ever state referendum on the issue." Funny that Sarah reports this in 2006 given that Missouri's shall-issue concealed carry law became effective on October 11, 2004. Really Sarah, can you pay your staff a little extra so they can keep your web site up to date … at least to the current century?

If picking on poor Sarah Brady seems too easy, then consider the Violence Policy Center's assertions on concealed carry. Their primary propaganda web page provides a summary, and attempts to extract cash in exchange for the full version of an ancient (1995) sewer of effluvium titled "Florida's Concealed Weapons Law – A Model for the Nation?" Instead of hurling a multitude of mendacities, the VPC attempts to scare the public with one concept: Criminals might want to carry handguns too. Josh Sugarmann is the only one surprised by this. Well, Sarah Brady was surprised too, given that her web site states that "many permit holders have been stripped of their permits for criminal behavior."

Sadly Sarah doesn't quantify "many," because doing so would illustrate the futility of her fervor. Thankfully, the VPC provides some numbers, but you have to dig to discern how they resemble the cited source data. Sugarmann's soldiers attempt to frighten voters in the remaining nine states that have not enacted concealed carry legislation through three related talking points:

- Criminals do apply for concealed carry licenses.
- Criminals do receive concealed carry licenses.
- Concealed carry license holders do commit crimes.

To which the average child would reply "duh!" Taken the common definition, we can assume that criminals will attempt to break laws, including laws forbidding them from obtaining a concealed carry permit. We can also easily imagine a government bureaucrat occasionally failing to caffeinate before coming into the office, and missing a reported conviction by a concealed carry applicant. Most importantly, when millions of people apply for a concealed carry permits it is thoroughly understandable if one or two eventually commit a crime. After all, people outside of the Kennedy Clan are not born criminals.

All Joshing aside, the VPC did ask the Florida Department of State, Division of Licensing for details on all the concealed carry permits that had been revoked from October of 1987 to May of 1995. What Josh's jesters discovered is indeed enlightening.

Of more than 200,000 licenses issued, 292 people (a bit more than one tenth of one percent) had their licenses revoked because they were convicted of a crime. Stated in a way foreign to the VPC, 99.9% of license holders did not commit any crimes more socially repugnant than failing to use their turn signals. Since violent crime is the whole reason people want to own guns or to ban them, knowing how many concealed carry license holders were convicted of firearm brutality is a key question, and one the VPC answers by burying the information deeply.

The number is five revoked licenses for violent crimes. That is 0.003% of issued permits. Even John Kerry achieved a higher body count in Vietnam, though friendly fire might have unfairly bumped up John's numbers. A few more Florida concealed carry licenses were revoked for petty theft and drug possession, crimes that barely warrant a written warning in Walla Walla.

In marketing there is an old adage that says "Don't believe your own hype." With concealed carry, only Sarah and Josh still buy the lies. Eighty percent of the states do not.

Oddly enough, neither does Dianne Feinstein. The same senator who jeopardized the lives of journalists, the one who candidly told a nationwide television audience that concerning handguns, "If I could have gotten 51 votes in the Senate of the United States for an outright [handgun] ban ... I would have done it," – she also had a California concealed carry permit, which is more rare than a San Francisco Republican. Feinstein was ahead of the national curve, having obtained her permit long before Florida made it virtually vulgus. Feinstein accepts the fact that packing heat is a damn good means of self-protection ... for Dianne (which is odder still considering she voted against interstate reciprocity for concealed carry permit holders like herself).

She should mention her carrying permit to Barack Obama. While chatting with his ideological soul mates at the Chicago Sun Times, Barack said, "There has not been any evidence that allowing people to carry a concealed weapon is going to make anyone safer." Maybe he'll take Feinstein's away.

# Chapter 3: The Children Who Never Were
(or how Michael Moores lie)

Hiding behind children never works for long. They are too small to be shields for plus sized adults.

Humans have a genetic predisposition to protect kids. If we had not acquired this trait long ago, our youngsters would have been eaten by various carnivores that are not picky about protein sources. Given the agonizingly long time span from childbirth to a child getting a cave of their own, there were ample opportunities for wildlife to chew on children before they could in turn create more children. Thus, normal human beings developed an autonomic response to defend their threatened broods in the interest of avoiding extinction.

All of which explains the Million Mom March, Michael Moore, and one of the greatest political put-ons ever fostered upon the drowsy American public.

Universal firearm registration has long been a primary goal of the gun control industry. As far back as 1976, Pete Shields, speaking as the chairman of the antecedent Handgun Control, Inc., listed registration as the middle step toward eliminating private firearm ownership – one step behind slowing overall handgun production, and one step ahead of total confiscation. Firearm registration is, after all, an essential element to firearm confiscation. Authorities would have a tough time rounding up several hundred million guns without a list of their last known locations. To achieve their publicly stated end game, various organizations have campaigned vigorously for firearm registration in state capitols and on Capitol Hill, with all the success of a Hillary Clinton presidential campaign.

Despite their efforts – or perhaps because of them – a weary American public did not buy into Pete Shield's registration scheme. Americans are an ornery lot, and have been distrustful of government ever since the days when Red Coat Target Practice was an entertaining pastime. With upwards of 53% of households owning a gun, and one or more guns available for every man, woman and hermaphrodite, Americans' innate suspicions about the need for and value of universal firearm registration were piqued by Shields' crusade. It seemed no amount of money, campaigning and posturing for "common sense" gun control overrode the collective common sense of the voting public. Indeed, if you asked yourself "what does licensing and registering guns have to do with criminal violence," you asked yourself the same question that a few million other folks did too.

So Sarah Brady and her coven began using children as targets.

**The Lie of Concern:** Demonstrating an insincere state of concern for others in order to achieve tangential objectives.

This form of falsity is particularly vexing to opponents, which is why politicians use it at every opportunity. Talk lovingly about tending to old folks, broadcast presidential thoughts about your cocker spaniel, and most especially hide behind children, and you garner immediate and deeply emotional connections with the vast majority of honorable and decent citizens, excluding of course honorable and decent cynics. For gun control advocates, the Lie of Concern conveniently created an insipient intersection between child welfare and firearm registration.

With registration proposals as intellectually dead as Friday night situation comedies, gun control lobbyists resorted to tugging on the innate emotions and survival instincts of the species, the one tactic with enough power to potentially overrun logic, patriotism and an equally innate loathing of Chuck Schumer. From within the fermenting bowels of the gun control movement gurgled forth the sound bite to end all sound bites – a canard so artfully crafted that it became the seed of a national spectacle as well as a pivotal campaign issue and the downfall of a presidential candidate.

"Thirteen children are murdered every day with handguns."

This single line achieves two accolades – one high, and one oh so very low. From a purely marketing standpoint, it was powerful phrase. It was short, easy to understand, and just as easy to repeat, which many a panting broadcast journalist did in blind earnest. It was mentally visual with the juxtaposition of children and handguns, bound by blood. Even the number thirteen was emotionally provocative given communal superstitions. Grudging compliments are bestowed on the copywriter who penned this line – it had traction in the political bazaar that Proctor & Gamble would envy in the laundry detergent market.

Selling bambino bloodshed for enactment of gun registration became the mission and mantra of the Million Mom March organization, and they were damn good. Backed by media-savvy operatives and some very deep pockets, the Million Mom March arose from the ashes of the Bell Campaign, so called given their Quasimodo-like fondness for ringing bells in self-indulgent displays of grief on behalf of the victims of violence (they prefer the term "gun violence," though I deeply suspect dead people are unconcerned about the specific means of their demise at the hands of criminal entrepreneurs). It is mildly entertaining to note the words of Beckie Brown, a member of the Bell Campaign Founders Council who, shortly before her organization morphed into non-existence, proclaimed, "We are not going away until we've accomplished what we set out to do." Given that recent local Million Mom March events turn out as few as ten participants, we can assume that they indeed have left the political stage.

But in that bacchanal of bravado known as the 2000 election cycle, the Million Mom March was out for blood, so to speak. They adopted the "13 children a day" slogan as their rallying cry. Broadcasting this sound bite was engineered by career professionals in the media trade such as Donna Dees-Thomases who, despite recently adopting the persona of a fretting housewife and mother, had media and political connections that made Rupert Murdoch salivate. Donna brought to the marching mommies a public-relations background that included stints working for Dan Rather at CBS News, and as Assistant Press Secretary to retired Senators Russell Long and Bennett Johnston. Such expertise was precisely what the Million Mom March needed to assure that the factitious "13 children a day" war cry was transmitted from every broadcast tower and aped by editors across the country.

Political positioning was manufactured in stride with Million Mom March imagery. Their web site, literature and logos reeked of anything child-and-mother related. Professional illustrators crafted colorful crayon cartoons reminiscent of both juvenile scribblings and cave drawings (perhaps cavemen's children drew on the walls like our own kinder, and archeologists have been misinterpreting the meaning of pictographs all along). The color pink was their brand anchor, as they fought to peel women away from the American voting pack as Dianne Feinstein had peeled "assault weapon" owners away from the gun-owning majority. Donna Dees-

Thomases portrayed herself as a typical suburban mom and someone who "never really organized anything larger than a car pool before." Most interestingly, Donna was called "a mother who'd never been politically active," which surprises everyone from her former Senate employers to her sister-in-law Susan Thomases, a long-time friend and political adviser to Hillary Clinton.

**The Lie of Camaraderie:** Portraying false associations with a person or organization to create an emotive bond.

Humans are pack animals, which is why dogs like us so much – to a dog, people are acceptable pack mates and equally acceptable substitutes for dogs. Humans create herds all the time, be they tribes, political parties or even virtual asylums like MoveOn.org. Corporations get consumers to emotionally connect with products by crafting affinity through cultural bonding. Beer brewers run advertisements touting "man laws" to emotionally affix males to otherwise tasteless suds. Pharmaceutical companies make erectile dysfunction look orgiastic and appeal to instincts baser than even beer guzzling. Each group attempts to create its own pack by coaxing connections in the gut, or some that reside a few centimeters lower.

Marketing the mommy angle for gun registration was no accident. Donna Dees-Thomases massaged instinctive connections that are the very bedrock of mankind through a campaign as authentic as Harry Reid's warmth. Hiding behind cribs, they erected a façade of motherly concern that barely masked a Machiavellian drive for firearm licensing and registration. Donna's marching moms attached themselves to raw maternal instinct, and crafted the best Lie of Camaraderie told since Hitler's Master Race corker.

Strategically brilliant as the media campaign was, it suffered from a single profound weakness – their "13 children a day" sound bite was an overflowing bucket of statistical excreta.

### The Lie of Statistics: The use of numbers that present misleading information and distort perspective.

Laurence J. Peter understood this principle when he said, "Facts are stubborn things, but statistics are more pliable." In politics, statistics and allegedly academic studies are used to create instant believability. Average homo sapiens lack the time, talent or tenacity to dig deeply into raked muck to find occasional pearls of truth. We all rely on seemingly plausible information from seemingly moral people to believe complete insanity. When a band of mothers – who through media manipulation appeared to spontaneously unite in maternal defense of children everywhere – cited credible *sounding* sources, an average adult might well be swayed into action. Since historically American men were more prone to gun ownership than their wives, girlfriends or temporal bed buddies, the Million Mom March ploy calculatedly targeted the other half of the population.

Thirteen was an unlucky number for the Million Mom March, because it was too easy to invalidate. One dirty secret of gun control political wars is that both sides use the same numbers. Raw data comes from the FBI, the Bureau of Justice Statistics, the National Safety Council and the Centers for Disease Control. Criminologists dice numbers very finely as they must communicate their findings to peers who will review their papers and crucify any research that is sloppy, politically incorrect or that contradicts what the reviewer has previously published. Political activists are not so careful and slice data sloppily, given that the average Joe or Jane lacks the necessary man-hours to excavate statistical sewage.

However, criminologists, who routinely sort through reams of such data, were a bit confounded by findings that concluded 13 children were murdered each day in America. Having previously spelunked the figures from which Donna's devils derived this particular perjury, criminologists instinctively knew something was wildly amiss. Given that working criminologists are paid to research such things, and that grading freshmen term papers is a snore, they delved into the "13 children a day" claim using the exact same sources as the Million Mom March.

What happened next was as comical as it was creepy. With each peel of the intellectual onion, various gun control groups revised their slogan. It started when a criminologist politely pointed out that the definition of murder was fairly strict. Given that about half of all firearm-related deaths in the United States are from suicides, it was highly unlikely that thirteen children were *murdered*. In fact, given the relatively low murder rate of children in general, regardless of the method, it was difficult to grasp from where the marching mom claim arose.

"Thirteen children die from guns each day" was what appeared in the next run of leaflets, web sites and on the lips of panting reporters for whom the change in phrasing was unobserved.

Criminologists are a tidy lot, inflicted with statistical obsessive/compulsive disorders. Each criminologist I meet fits our stereotype of a nerdy number cruncher. Being wholly and severely anal retentive, they were unhappy with the Marching Moms' revised carnage claim and drilled deeper to make an interesting discovery – that the dead "children" tallied in these reports might be as old as 24. Granted, some early-twenties drug-dealing thug may be somebody's "baby," but he certainly is no *child*. Criminologists and lexicographers alike pointed out that a "child" is one who has not yet breached puberty, with the commonly accepted age being thirteen. The gun control industry had intentionally included children who routinely hung out in bars, gambled and had sex with the President. Their list held almost as many people past the point of puberty as were below it.

"Thirteen *young people* are killed by gun violence each day" was the new boilerplate, and television talking heads mumbled through their revised teleprompter prose with only a modicum of confusion.

Several new issues instantly came to the lips of criminologists, who gun control activists were now willing to shoot. Two intertwined issues revolved around the robust industry of gangland warfare. Government reports and various sociological studies note that gangs and related drug trafficking are responsible for a upwards of 94% of firearm homicides each year, and that gangs have recruited children as young as seven. Some portion of gangland deaths were teens already recruited into gangs, as were a number of innocents hit by stray bullets intended for their drug-dealing "uncles." This inconvenient fact caused Donna's dastards massive heartburn as they faced having to explain the difference between criminals – who were very unlikely to accommodate the government by registering their (typically stolen) firearms – and average American gun owners who wanted to keep these same thugs out of their homes.

You might think that criminologists would have stopped after three separate revelations of Million Mom March myth-making. After all, how much fun and frivolity can someone intimate using standard deviations? Criminologists are apparently indefatigable, and there is a certain momentum that develops when a researcher gets his or her nose buried too deeply into statistical tables. Researchers simply had to remind the media that some firearm deaths are accidental, and not from violent malevolence. The number was small – only 72 people under age 15 died from firearm accidents in 2001 (the Center for Disease Control divides mortality age data between 14 and 15 years of age, whereas the FBI divides crime data between 13 and 14, just to make things tough for researchers). Yet these accidental deaths were included in the original estimates fabricated by the gun control lobby. Social scientists asked for corrections.

"Thirteen young people are killed by guns each day" was the gun control industry's perseverate response before the election of 2000, and even the most inattentive of television reporters started asking Donna to "get your frickin' story straight!"

The decline, demise and final absorption of the Million Mom March into Sarah Brady's group was facilitated by stripping away the thinning veneer Donna Dees-Thomases created. Women were far from unified on this topic, which was the fatal flaw of the "commie mommy" strategy. As women became increasingly independent throughout the late 20th century, they also became less protected. Attacked by rapists, sadistic ex-husbands, and largely ignored by politicians holding police budgets for ransom, women had gradually armed themselves in both self-defense and the defense of their children. When the likes of Donna Dees-Thomases and Rosie O'Donnell proclaimed that they spoke for all women, many ladies replied "bunk!" (ladies being too polite to say "BS"). Where members of the Million Mom March met, members of the Second Amendment Sisters arrived. When camera crews came to the Oakland, California Million Mom March rally, they interviewed Mary Nelson, a local NRA volunteer activist as often as they interviewed Laurie Leiber, the Bay Area's Million Mom March publicist.

The Lie of Association fell apart on national television on May 12, 2000, two days before Mother's Day and the scheduled Million Mom March extravaganza. On ABC's Good Morning America, in a special Town Hall Meeting, another woman intellectually cornered the President of the United States in his Lie of Concern. Women from the Million Mom March, the NRA and other polarized groups met with the President to discuss gun control and the proposed licensing and registration ruse. Throughout the give and take, Bill Clinton echoed the themes of the Million Mom March media advisors, always harping on the child protection gambit. With each verbal maneuver, Clinton artfully tied his concocted concerns to the need for more laws to limit access to firearms.

Yet two women herded Clinton into a rhetorical cattle pen and branded his intellectually bare backside before a televised world audience.

The first blow to the Arkansas Ego came from Suzanna Hupp. Hupp had a front-row seat at the slaughter of 24 people, including her parents, at Luby's Cafeteria. By force of law, Hupp's handgun was legally secured in her glove compartment since Texas legislation in 1991 disallowed her to carry it concealed in public places such as Luby's. Like little Marion Hammer in Florida, Hupp became the marshalling force that passed concealed carry legislation in her state, to ensure that her fellow Lone Star ladies would not suffer as she had. Before a nationwide audience, Hupp described how the law prevented her from protecting her parents and 22 other people from mass murder, which brought to the prefrontal lobes of Americans the quaint idea that shooting bad guys might make good public policy.

Clinton's variation of the Lie of Concern was rapidly shattered. Blithely he ignored Hupp's point that an armed citizen might well prevent homicide. Knowing that a full frontal confrontation with a woman was a mistake – especially given his previously full frontal activities with female interns – Clinton began evasive maneuvers, trying to change the subject away from crime and toward accidental death.

"There is no law that covers every set of facts," Clinton said dismissively. "However, what the truth is in most instances, is that a lot of people have guns who don't know how to use them. And the accidental death rate in America is ... In America, I will say again – *forget about the crimes*, just look at the accidental gun rate."

President Clinton was then blindsided by Susan Howard, an actress, NRA member and another ornery Texas gal. With professional pacing that pushed Clinton into a box tighter than his human humidors, Howard exposed this particular Lie of Concern.

"Mr. President, I really have to ask you something," she said with a tiny, but well placed dramatic pause. "You just made the statement that just sent shivers up and down my spine. You said, let's forget the crimes and ..."

A visibly red and flustered Clinton stiffened and interrupted.

"No ..."

"No, no, no, sir, excuse me ...."

Sensing that his lack of concern was now more exposed than his carnal hiring criteria, Clinton turned to the Lie of Association and used the often vilified National Rifle Association as a proxy, blaming them for his own misstatement.

"This is the way the NRA operates," Clinton said with an unusual lack of force.

"No, sir, it's not. No, sir ..."

"All I did is – I don't want to forget the crimes ..."

"No, sir, you said, *let's forget the crime* and talk about the accidents – because there is nobody that ..."

"You know that's not what I meant, to forget the crime, Ms. Howard."

"But that's what you *said*, Mr. President."

For Bill Clinton, the President of the United States, the alleged leader of the free world (or the leader of the alleged free world), the debate rapidly spiraled out of his control. His sputtering responses instantly became the symbol of the dichotomy dividing the gun control movement, their sundry fabrications and a more reasoned American populace. His feigned concern for crime victims – much like his previously displayed lack of concern for grand jury testimony – led undecided voters to assume that he possessed no *authentic* concern. This and his past indiscretions led women across the country to believe he lacked the capacity for camaraderie with the other sex, the very souls the Million Mom March was desperately trying to cull. Combined, these factors cast doubt on the already weak foundation of the Million Mom March's statistical subterfuge.

Bill Clinton was the worst thing to happen to the gun control movement since Samuel Colt.

The political event of the year, and perhaps the decade, passed like last night's three bean casserole, with a pungent yet whispering breeze. Women were visibly divided on the issue, despite Hillary Clinton and Donna Dees-Thomases' claims of universal alignment. The "13 children a day" snaky statistic was dismissed or depreciated by the average voter, and even by the media before Father's Day neckties were safely concealed from public sight. Many mothers fond of self-protection became overnight celebrities, having gone toe-to-toe with the President of the United States, and as a result advancing the idea that women should consider buying a gun themselves. Yet the Million Mom Madness marched right along to election day, dragging to their political deaths a number of office holders who echoed their slouchy stats, with Al Gore being the most notable among the fallen. In the waning months of the 2000 election cycle, George Soros was listed as being the major financier of the marching moms, which raised the suspicions of every politically aware person. Though not yet a household name, "King George" as he is unaffectionately known, created increased scrutiny of Donna's organization, both because of his political alignment and because of an untidy insider trading conviction. Investigatory activity centered on Million Mom March financial records and filings. Rapidly, the last pieces of trim flew off the Million Mom March carriage as they were rocked by evidence of bending tax laws for non-profit (and allegedly non-political) organizations, and as they were tossed out of government-financed digs in San Francisco. Before another year passed, what was left of the Marching Moms was quietly acquired by the Brady Center to Prevent Gun Violence. Like a criminally errant child coming home, Mother Sarah took in the bedraggled waif before the IRS could toss its keister in jail.

And yet, to this day, the Million Mom March exists and promotes pretty much what they have from the start. Today their web pages show photographs of mothers cuddling cherubs with exploding cheeks and playful eyes. These images swap over one another, painting portraits that scream "motherly love," only to be replaced with a black-on-pink banner stating "8 children are killed every day in America by guns."

Some people never learn. One of these people is Michael Moore.

With a well polished "aw shucks" demeanor that even his employers at Mother Jones couldn't stomach for long, Michael latched leech-like onto one of the most atypical episodes in American history where firearms and kids intersected. The Columbine Massacre was custom made for Moore's particular brand of propaganda. Littleton's murdered children created an emotional shield large enough for even the Rubenesque Moore to hide behind.

With a nascent election cycle gurgling on the horizon, a sitting president looking for a legacy that did not include cigars and interns, and a nearly rabid gun control organization flush with King George's insider trading profits, Columbine's dead kids became building bricks for gun control advocates. Battle cries claiming that America's "lax gun laws" were solely to blame for twelve dead students rose from pundits, talking heads, Sarah, Donna, and of course Michael's lips between feeding frenzies.

Lost in rhetorical rampages over registration of handguns was the fact that Eric Harris and Dylan Klebold, the Columbine killers, attempted carnage using every method two screwball schoolboys could scrounge. They experimented with pipe bombs, rigged propane tanks to blast, and even tried cooking a batch of napalm. On their D-day, two propane tanks with enough explosive assertiveness to bring down a building were deposited in the school's cafeteria, set to detonate when the first lunch shift of students would be busily wolfing down fries and chattering about the basketball team's win/loss record. Only Harris and Klebold's engineering ineptitude kept the Columbine body count from climbing into the hundreds.

Gun control activists buried these details as deeply as cats bury litter box misdeeds. They diverted media attention away from the intent of Harris and Klebold to murder buildings full of people, and onto the more visible and visceral fact that the one type of weapon that actually worked for these junior loons was a couple of guns. Yet Josh, Donna, Sarah and their swarm did not clamor over two shotguns that were responsible for most of the dead coeds (Harris blasted his 25 times), or the rifle that was more accurate and powerful. They focused on the handguns. Grainy lunchroom videos of Harris and Klebold toting menacing-looking little Tec-9 pistols were recurrently broadcast by a palpitating media while gun control front men and women pouted, proclaiming how "common sense" licensing and registration would have prevented this tragedy.

Out of courtesy we must assume they meant licensing and registration of BBQ grill propane tanks.

People with utopian notions about a gun-free America seized upon Columbine, knowing viscerally the emotive nature of the event. All forms of political lies were manifested, from Sarah Brady perfecting the Lie of Fear, to Bill Clinton milking the Lie of Omission, telling the American electorate that guns needed to be registered but concubines and Cohibas did not. Yet a suspicious public was unwilling to swallow the hook, much less the line and sinker. The logical disconnect between anti-depressant activated assassinations committed by two asinine adolescents, and every American who kept a peacemaker in their night stand was plainly obvious to everyone except Diane Sawyer. What the gun control lobby lacked was a voice that spoke with sway and swagger, with journalistic jurisdiction and good-natured guts.

What they got was Michael Moore, who in the absence of a sane documentarian, would simply have to suffice.

**The Lie of Authority:** To speak with authority, though not fact, and by such presence keep others from questioning the information.

Nobody since Goebbels has perfected the Lie of Authority better than Moore. Through repeated insistence that his hired fact-checkers vet every verb used in his books and films, to bold (though behind the camera) confrontations, Moore bolsters his ego and self-manufactured image of a skilled and scrupulous chronicler of truth, and in "Bowling for Columbine" as a defender of America's children. These are essential ingredients in the Lie of Authority, for the moment the fat lady's voice waivers, the Internet's political opera society is poised to critique.

And strike they did, with the ruthless efficiency that only a few hundred bored people with too much time on their hands can muster. Within hours of the first public screening of "Bowling for Columbine," the ether of the Ethernet was abuzz with exchanged insights that plopped between incredulous disbelief at Moore's pure chutzpah, and point-by-point dissections of errant misinformation throughout the film. This thicket of factual iniquities finally grew so large that when Moore received an Oscar for the film as the year's best documentary, some members of the Academy of Motion Picture Arts and Sciences insisted that the award be revoked to preserve the sanctity of the Academy.

And of the word "documentary." Lexicographers can be an ornery bunch, because unlike Michael, they rely on accuracy.

Moore committed the one sin that Liars of Authority can never perpetrate: He allowed easily detectable, yet significant deceits into his work. "Bowling for Columbine" opens with the assertion that Harris and Klebold, members of Columbine High School's bowling league, had indeed gone bowling the morning of the massacre, though quickly fact-checking interviews with the police or the other members of the school's gutter-ballers would have shown that Columbine's executioners had skipped that morning's recreational activities. Later, Moore assembled a montage in which he receives a hunting rifle in exchange for opening a thousand-dollar savings account in Michigan that was allegedly arranged in advance to get past bureaucratic delays, yet portrays the transaction as "cash and carry." This canard was facilitated in part by omitting film of the on-site presentation of photo identification and any requisite background checks. Moore goes as far as to blame the United States government for giving $245 million to Afghanistan's Taliban regime (it actually went to international humanitarian relief agencies) and punctuates his point with stock footage of the World Trade Center in flames.

**The Lie of Context:** Showing either a small snippet alone, or a string of snippets together, to create a false impression of what happened.

All these inaccuracies might be minor or debatable. Creating an entire multi-million dollar convention and tradeshow out of thin air is not. Therein, Moore is as ballsy as a brahma bull. He chose to demonize gun owners by proxy, and to make the NRA appear indifferent to the Columbine catastrophe, by bringing to Denver an event that never occurred.

Years before Harris and Klebold concocted their on-campus ambush, the NRA had scheduled its annual business meeting and members' convention for Denver, Colorado, of which Littleton is a suburb and Columbine High School is a satellite. NRA members, firearm manufactures, bullet makers, apparel vendors, hunting scope craftsmen and the typical annual mob had far in advance paid their registration fees, rented their booths and bought airplane tickets for the Queen City of the Plains – a nickname Denver should drop unless they intend to rob San Francisco of a voting block. Like every annual convention from every year before, the NRA coterie was expected to bring convention revenues to Denver, which in exchange only had to contend with a throng of boring middle-aged masses overrunning an otherwise colorful downtown in May.

But Hitler's 110th birthday party came to Columbine on April 20, besting the NRA's pre-planned event by less than a month. Charlton Heston and his crew cut the legislatively mandated members' business meeting from three days down to one, canceled after-meeting festivities, had local billboard advertisements removed from sight in Denver, and most expensively, scrapped the tradeshow that would have coated 170,000 square feet of convention space, sending more than 350 vendors home with millions of dollars in refunds. Charlton Heston apologized to the NRA members who did show up expecting a full monty of shooting sport entertainment by saying, "As you know, we've cancelled the festivities, the fellowship we normally enjoy at our annual gatherings. This decision has perplexed a few and inconvenienced thousands. As your president, I apologize for that." Rumor has it that the NRA even contemplated canceling the business meeting altogether, only to discover that New York law – the governing law of NRA's state of incorporation – required the meeting to be held. For the sake of local sensitivities, the NRA lost a lot of time, money and momentum in the political realm thanks to simple bad timing and two losers on antidepressant-withdrawal enhanced self-induced rage.

Pity that Michael Moore's crack team of fact-checkers missed these subtleties.

**The Lie of Non Sequiturs:** Combining vaguely related, or completely unrelated, information to create a false impression or conclusion.

"Bowling for Columbine" presents a sequence of footage that was either inspired mastery or a byproduct of a mental breakdown. The montage jumps from footage of children (remember, Michael is using kids for camouflage) outside of Columbine High School to Charlton Heston hoisting an antique musket overhead and reciting his now famous "From my cold, dead hands" script. Before we see Heston speaking again, there are flashes of the billboard that the NRA had posted in Denver well before the massacre, and Moore's non-melodious voice, soggy with insincere regret, saying "Just ten days after the Columbine killings, despite the pleas of a community in mourning, Charlton Heston came to Denver and held a large pro-gun rally for the National Rifle Association." Footage resumes with Heston addressing an absent Mayor of Denver.

Moore's intent is as transparent as the reality it purposefully fails to portray. Moore paints the NRA and gun owners as insensitive louts through careful omission of what the NRA did in reaction to the Columbine killings – removing billboards and canceling almost all pre-paid events – and through stitching together footage shot a year apart and in reverse order.

Yes, the opening scene of Heston lifting a firearm not used since the 18th century and daring the government to lock up his flintlock was taken a year after Columbine, in a city on the other side of the country. Moore used film that was not shot in Denver, was not taken in the same year as the Columbine massacre, and before an audience that wasn't anywhere near Denver. Either Michael Moore has perfected time travel, or Moore's team of researchers needs to review the time stamps on his video tapes.

If Moore was willing to time-shift footage to perjure for his politics, few people would be surprised that he was also willing to splice together audio to defame his enemies; the rest of us fully expect it. Interspersing clips from more than one speech, and injecting unrelated images in between, Heston's remarks about fighting for his country, about the freedom of people to travel as they please, and about NRA members who were in the SWAT team that responded to the calls of panic from Columbine were morphed into an otherworldly impression that Chuck Heston had told Denver's mayor to shove it a mile high up his rump. Moore did much the same elsewhere in "Bowling for Columbine" by insinuating that the NRA and the Ku Klux Klan were created in the same year (the KKK was founded five years earlier) by the same people (the Klan was founded by former slave-owning rednecks, and the NRA was founded by an abolitionist general of the Union army). Some cynics have openly wondered why Moore did not splice footage of NRA frontman Wayne LaPierre having carnal relations with Satan while eating live puppies, for that was about as plausible as what Moore actually provided.

Political huckstering is all about the "saveables," the swing voters. Politicos preach to the saints, arming agreeable people with ample argumentative hyperbole with which to engage the enemy. It doesn't matter if it is all fakery and deceit, the faithful will flail onward with whatever weapons are provided. Politicos also preach to the sinners, those they oppose, to create uncertainty and doubt. But most of all political war lords assail the yet unswayed, to predispose their biases until documentable or self-evident fact, or the very voice of God tells them otherwise. Such is propaganda, and such is the motivation to use innocent children as emotional pawns in political maneuvering. Lies crafted to seemingly protect children are reflexively adopted. So Josh Sugarmann, Donna Dees-Thomases, Sarah Brady, millions of misguided moms, and the ever-expanding Michael Moore lift unendangered children as their shields when marching into battle, for we dare not strike the children themselves.

It is a simple charade, one so simple that even the Academy of Motion Picture Arts and Sciences may one day see the light of day – eclipsed only temporarily by Michael Moore's girth – and revoke his ill-gotten Oscar.

One could lay to rest the discussion of children and "young people," and the entire Million Mom March mask as an exercise in political warfare and excess, if it were not for Barbara Graham, a Million Mom March organizer, spokesperson and convicted shooter.

Barbara, a resident of Washington D.C. who saddled up with Rosie O'Donnell to speak to the assembled mob on Mother's Day, later gunned down an innocent man using a Tec-9, a banned "assault weapon" and one of several handguns found in her house. The man she shot is now permanently paralyzed, Graham is in jail, and the Million Mom March makes not a single mention of this on their web site.

# Chapter 4: The Bureaucracy That Never Worked
(or how Michael Beards lie)

Similarities between drug-addled bums and gun control advocates are oddly striking.

I exited the Powell subway station in the center of San Francisco's Market Street district and proceeded to walk up to my favorite walk-down blues bar. The sidewalks were littered with a typical assortment of vagabonds in various stages of intoxication and hallucinogenic rapture. One particularly vigorous vagrant approached, hand thrust forward in a belligerent fundraising style heretofore unknown outside of the Illinois Governor's office. Lapsing judgment caused me to slip a dollar into his hand, while avoiding actual physical contact. Encouraged, he followed me up Powell Street, at first talking about money, then cops, then space aliens, abductions, globalization, the "shadow government" and finally his Grand Unified Conspiracy Theory. At the height of his fevered oration, he grabbed my shoulder – my *good* jacket at that – and shouted in wide-eyed certainty, "Don't you see? It's *common sense!*"

That afternoon on television, Hillary Clinton said, "We have to do more to stand up to those who refuse to believe ... that ... *common sense* gun measures can make a difference."

Contrasting individual lunatics is inappropriate, but these coincidences of speech illuminate a profligate and pungent prevarication.

### The Lie of Invalidatable Conclusions: Pronouncing with certainty what has never been and can never be proven.

Demented panhandlers and delusional Senators, presidential candidates and Secretaries of State share more than mere oratorical tendencies. By substituting opinion as a foregone conclusion, and doing so with rum- or regency-induced conviction, one can infect weaker minds with the same assumptions. It helps if one is not manic, and thus the panhandler has an advantage over the politician.

The phrase "common sense" was hijacked by the gun control industry and puppeteered during the Million Mom March campaign of 2000. The careful marketing of motherly images and parental-sounding "common sense" slogans were designed to reinforce the Lie of Invalidatable Conclusions in a "mother knows best" emotive montage. During that year many "common sense gun measures" were whelped, weaned, fattened and eventually sacrificed on Utopia's alter. Central to prohibitionist pandemonium (the Place of All the Demons) were the paired horns of handgun licensing and registration and the recurring lie that these panacea were of value to anyone aside from the pressman who printed Million Mom March flyers, a fellow last seen sipping champagne in the Lincoln Bedroom.

Marching moms and presidential wannabes repeated the same claims, with enough variations to doom their own messaging. Distilled, their claims were:

1) Licensing will improve gun owner safety.

2) Registration will catch criminals who use guns.

Many in the media repeated the "common sense" phrase like drunken parrots falling off their ink-stained bar stools. Though passing journalistic analysis, each claim failed actual scrutiny, historical assessment and sober reflection. Cynics and other experienced thinkers knew there was less than met the eye when children were paraded like moving targets in the crosshairs of "common sense" assertions. As with mythical "assault weapons", the claim of improving the state of the world first required assuming that the world was in a bad way – that accidental shootings were dropping gun-owner family members faster than pills are dropped at a Don Imus vacation retreat. It also assumed that criminals would obey firearm registration laws before heading off to work, where their job descriptions oddly included the task of breaking laws.

Licensing gun owners for sake of improving safety is like entering the priesthood to improve celibacy. Despite there being at least one firearm for every man, woman and transsexual in America, the rate of accidental annihilation from firearms is low and has fallen steadily without the aid of congressional oversight. In the year 2000, out of all Americans – from the cradle to those past due for the grave – only 776 were mistakenly shot to death, ranking a measly 0.8% of all fatal accidents (this barely detectible rate may well be inflated as many "accidents" have suspicious circumstances). The year 2000 was no exception in that regard because the rate of lethal firearm flukes had plunged 59% in the two preceding decades despite a steadily growing accumulation of private firepower.

Well-armed Americans are at less risk than gerbils during Pride week.

This state of safe affairs caused consternation within the gun control industry. It is difficult to incite a mob without a monster, and adults are quick to accept a certain amount of dangerous adult stupidity as long as the loss of life is confined to the shooter or his crack-smoking buddies. Victimized children are a different matter. Extremely rare but extremely well broadcast stories of innocents being slain by irresponsible "adults" arouses everybody's sympathies outside of the Al Qaeda home office. To achieve universal handgun licensing, gun control advocates had to link chronically low accidental firearm death rates with yet another "save the children" campaign. Your heart strings remain unplucked when you only picture members of the Crips accidentally reinforcing their brand upon themselves through projectile exchange parties.

One group within the gun control industry was so artful in their message development that they managed to weave together these two disjointed topics into seamless and reprehensible whole cloth:

> *Our children must be protected! With almost 1,000 deadly firearm accidents this year alone ...*

Anyone intelligent enough to not work in the CBS News research department sees the contradiction within these piled populations – that children are a subset of all those accidentally killed. Yet the orchestrated sound bite brought to the public mind images of 1,000 dead toddlers stacked in a corporal mass by the teeter-totters. Since most people live outside of American inner city shooting galleries, or far from the lead showers raining down during Cinco de Mayo, very few folk personally experience a fledgling fatality, and with good reason given the order of magnitude gap between numbers 776 and 86.

Lamentable it is that 86 children – actual pre-pubescent children and not the 24–year-old gang bangers the Million

Mom March tallied – were accidentally killed with firearms in 2000. But to give some perspective, that is less than two children in each state of the Union, and 0.0001% of the children residing therein. Even this low number may have been semantically inflated given that "accidental firearm fatalities" include all forms of unintended demise including stay bullets in drive-by shootings and vice presidential hunting trips.

Finicky criminologists, this time joined by persnickety public health statisticians, managed to find a few cub reporters under the legal drinking age. They complained that the bloody portraits painted by gun control advocates was somewhere between distorted and delusional. Inconvenient questions surfaced at Brady and Million Mom March events. Panicked, the gun control industry shifted their registration and licensing story from one of a *common sense* need to protect children to one of utterly irrational equivalency.

They equated guns with cars.

Nearly everyone of voting age drives. Sure, some humans are hopelessly trapped in the hopelessly urban jungle of Manhattan, enjoying bumper car rides courtesy of suicidal taxi drivers who are automatically issued cab licenses upon entry into the country. Some people do not drive because they have reached an age so advanced that the government – in a rare instance of lucidity – defends the lives and safety of the public by yanking driver licenses from wrinkled hands before cerebral strokes cause grandparents to pilot a ton of Detroit steel into the local farmers market. A nearly universal association with the need for an automobile and government oversight of publicly using automobiles made for a convenient canard in proposing handgun licensing and registration through:

**The Lie of Invalid Policy Comparisons:** Comparing two seeming similar policies so the rational effects of one are inappropriately associated with the other.

Gun control industry marketing departments soon oozed another sound bite. Office holders loved to repeat the line because parroting the phrase reinforced their self-aggrandizing illusions of being both smarter and in charge. Licensing of gun owners was associated with licensing drivers. Attempts were made to pacify firearm owners, suggesting that the rigors of being allowed to own guns – objects already owned without previous government permission – would be as easy as getting a driver's license.

Obviously nobody at the Brady Campaign has spent an afternoon in line at the DMV.

This inane analogy – *prima facie inconcinnus* – was extended to cover firearm registration, comparing registering your revolver to registering your ride. Perhaps if we carried our revolvers into the DMV, workers there would be more polite and the line would speed up a bit.

Ignoring for a moment the very real issue of constitutional rights and the inappropriate licensing thereof, we encounter an inexplicable comparison of bizarre bent. Public roads are owned by (surprise) the public. The public, being empowered by ownership to regulate use of their collective property, call upon their elected employees to enact whatever laws are necessary to keep highway holocausts to a minimum. But a person's home is private *property* and oddly immobile, incapable of giving your insurance adjuster ulcers after you slam your three bedroom rancher into the Dutch colonial model down the street. Thus licensing the ownership of private property (your firearm) for storage within another piece of private property (your home) has little resemblance to licensing jalopy jockeys rocketing through schoolyard crosswalks. It has about as much resemblance as Nancy Pelosi has to Raquel Welch, or any woman for that matter.

Invalid comparisons cause headaches when *idee fixe* intersects with political science. The gun control industry suggested that registering guns was the moral equivalent of registering SUVs. This comparison suffered from the same fallacy as licensing firearm-owners, namely the conundrum of public versus private. The logical gulf was so wide that even Rosie O'Donnell could not rhetorically leap it – though unimaginable is the thought she could leap anything aside from the line of an all-you-can-eat buffet.

The Lie of Invalid Comparison suffers from one distinct problem: It invites comparison, which in turn invites mockery. Gun rights advocates seized upon the automobile angle and publicly replied that *they agreed with the concept* – gun owners wanted the systems to be exactly the same. This befuddled Sarah Brady, Josh Sugarmann and Chuck Schumer long enough for the other side to find and infect the thinking of some media members. Gun owner arguments went something like this:

> There is no legal limit on how many cars I can own.

> There is no restriction on what kinds of vehicles I can own – motorcycles, cars, trucks, semis, limos, armored personnel carriers.

> I can use a car any way I like as long as I keep it on my own property.

> I can take my car wherever I go in public, throughout all 50 states, and all I must first do is take a test.

Applied to firearms this translated into:

> No one-gun-a-month or "arsenal" limits.

> I can own "assault weapons," machine guns, bazookas and tactical jet fighters with ordnance.

I can turn my backyard into a rifle range.

And I get to pack heat wherever I want,
whenever I want, from coast to coast and
border to border after answering some
questions on a quiz.

Needless to say the gun control industry had not thought of
this because, as has been demonstrated, they are incapable of
thinking without assistance from an advertising agency. True
to form their agencies pondered their failed sound bite for an
afternoon and reconstructed their deception into a turbid
"crime control" argument, the gist of which was that universal
firearm registration would be a boon to law enforcement
everywhere, making every gun found at a crime scene traceable to the criminal who used it. They asserted that immediately after universal registration was enacted, the streets
would be cleared of gun-toting thugs.

Finished laughing? Good. We'll continue.

Inquisitive criminologists had long wondered where felons
acquired their guns. After all, walking into a neighborhood
gun store and risking arrest when the FBI's Instant Background Check spews forth your rap sheet is stupid even by a
criminal's low standards (though it does pass intellectual
muster within Urban League offices). While pondering the
problem, criminologists stumbled across a valuable reality –
that felons sentenced to life without parole had little to fear by
telling the truth. For decades hence criminologists have been
breaking into jail to interview, survey and mentally molest
inmates with the intent of discovering many interesting and
helpful insights: Why did they become criminals? How did
they get caught? Where did they get their guns? Did this
affect their chance at reelection?

As far back as the 1980s a provocative trend developed.
Criminologists saw that most guns used in felonies – as many
as four in five – were stolen, be it from the home of a vaca-
tioning couple, from a hijacked delivery truck or from parked

cop cars. Somewhere between the theft of the firearm and it being recovered from a crime scene, enterprising scofflaws typically filed away the serial numbers, making the gun untraceable. Grinding off serial numbers is so prevalent an act, it routinely makes its way into television crime dramas and other intellectual septic systems. Hence firearm registration for crime control defies the very "common sense" that gun control proponents feign.

Such weak rhetoric and weaker thinking was unnecessary. Since firearms have been under mandatory registration in several states and many nations for an extended period of time, by theory there was a long list of crimes that were resolved by tracing registered rods. All Sarah Brady had to do was call up constables in New York or Maryland or the United Kingdom and get hard, statistical proof of the effectiveness of firearm registration for locating criminal offenders.

Which explains why she didn't. They didn't phone New Zealand, which canned its program after NZ police found it "worthless." They didn't call Australia, a country that spends around $200,000,000 annually on their system though their Chief Inspector called the country's crime prevention capabilities "a fallacy." They didn't even bother to call Canada where the gun registration system – which runs more than 1,646% over budget – "… has neither deterred these crimes nor helped us solve any," according to the Toronto police chief. Nor did the gun control industry call Hawaii, Chicago or Washington D.C., where despite decades of registration and even outright bans, the system has yet to identify a single criminal via firearm registration. Brady and company may be perjurers, but they are bright enough not to pee in their own porridge.

Intrinsic to their publicity campaigns, the gun control industry relies (or re-lies) on multiple deceptions to peddle its particular poisons. Information technology has proven useful in convincing consumers (influenced by Google's massive database) or citizens (haunted by never-ending jury duty notices) to accept gun registration as viable. Such omniscient digital warehouses make registration schemes seem practical by irrational comparison.

**The Lie of Big Databases:** Claiming that sufficiently large databases will instantly identify useful information.

The concept is instinctively appealing. Force everyone who makes or owns a firearm to register the serial number into a huge, centralized database. Track the gun through any sales, inheritances or horse trading between friends. When a gun is used in a crime, simply look up the last registered owner and slap the cuffs on him.

Simple, elegant, inane.

Chief of Police Dan Wesson (not his real name) has gone against official policy and allowed me to rummage around the evidence room of his department. Since Wesson runs the cop shop for a moderately large California city, the room is actually a small warehouse. A corner of his cavern holds guns allegedly used in crimes. There are a couple of illegally abbreviated shotguns. I found one of Dianne Feinstein's mythical "assault weapons." Mostly I see handguns, the tool of choice for common street thugs.

With gloved hands I pick up three at random. I examine their age (moderately old), condition (horrible) and serial number. Actually, I inspect deep grooves carved by bench grinders where the serial numbers once were. I select three more guns, and find three more cases of assault by power tools.

"Pretty normal," says Wesson. "We don't find many with traceable markings." I ask him how many crime guns he has been able to trace to California's registration database. Chief Wesson stared at me as if something were growing out of my head before touching the tip of his thumb and index finger to form a *zero*.

Missing in the gun control industry's alleged calculus is the division between criminals and you (and if you are a criminal, put down this book, drop to your knees and put your hands behind your head). The Lie of Big Databases is crippled by the fact that it holds only data for those people who have opted to obey the law and register their firearms. If your personal crime spree consists of cheating on your diet, odds are you would register your guns. A pack of MS-13 gang members who lead-pipe a UPS deliveryman and swipe a box of handguns headed for a federally licensed gun store are somewhat less likely to register them.

Nor are they legally obligated to do so. The U.S. Supreme Court ruled that no felon can be compelled to register the guns they are not allowed to own because doing so violates their Fifth Amendment rights against self-incrimination.

Of course law abiding people can choose to resist registration schemes and in effect become part of the unelected criminal class. If firearm registration in other countries is an indicator, registration fails to get participation from previously law abiding people. Germany estimates that 80% of firearms were never registered. In Canada, 20,000 citizens revolted against their government's late-20th-century registration scheme by publicly announcing they would not participate, and it is assumed many times that number refused silently. Residents of Boston and Cleveland allegedly have a 1% compliance rate and the California State Senate Committee on Judiciary concluded that a mere 10% of Golden State residents bother with some firearms.

We could expect registration rates in Texas to be negative.

The gun control industry must be given credit for pit bull tenacity as well as demeanor. Sensing such wide-scale resistance, they devised different angles to perpetuate fear and instill in undecided voters the desire to "do something" regardless of how useless that something might be. Key in its ongoing efforts to frighten the fainthearted, the gun control industry relies on big numbers as well as big databases. Any seemingly large figure, improperly positioned, causes incautious voters to react and enact. The bigger the number, the more scared the citizen.

> **The Lie of Proportion:** Avoid show-
> ing relative proportions in order to
> avoid showing the weakness of an ar-
> gument.

To enact any form of gun control, the industry must make voters believe that the world is out of control. The Lie of Big Databases inverts such fear by asserting that a massive collection of data can overwhelm thousands of thugs with over 150 years of experience in removing serial numbers off of guns (interesting it is that both Al Qaeda and the Bloods use low-tech methods to defeat high-tech protections). To sell any protection plan, the perception of a problem must first exist (Brinks Home Security services runs television commercials of tough-looking characters breaking into homes for a reason). Large, disconnected numbers effectively induce fear and thus the gun control industry assiduously submits one scary figure after another without providing perspective. Perspective is more dangerous to Hillary Clinton's gun control designs than her STD-laden hubby is to her. Hillary can't avoid perspective, but she doesn't have to boink Billy.

"Thirty thousand people were killed with guns in America last year" is a favorite gun control sound bite. Thirty thousand people would fill a small football stadium. Twelve thousand wouldn't. Three thousand would not fill a Kennedy compound liquor cabinet. But 3,000 might actually be the important number.

The 30,000 death-by-gun myth includes nearly 17,000 suicides. Since suicide rates do not change with or without the availability of a gun, at worst we have 13,000 deaths to fret over. Yet "firearm deaths" have a number of causes including accidents (south of 700 in 2004) and "legal interventions," or justifiable/meritorious shootings (north of 300). When whittled down we see something less than 12,000 homicides using a gun. This seems like a lot of manslaughter until one examines who pulls the trigger. The Bureau of Justice Statistics – a place too sober to interest reporters – notes that nearly 80% of all homicides and 94% of gun homicides are gang related. Various criminological studies show that upwards of 80% of homicides are committed by repeat violent offenders, and the same unsavory people travel in both groups – inner-city imbeciles running in gangs and running drugs.

These are also the same fellows who grind serial numbers off of their unregistered, stolen guns.

The unexposed perspective – one buried deeper than ACORN's second set of books – is that 94% of the preventable firearm homicides are committed by as few as 3,000 well-known career criminals. The bulk of America's so-called handgun violence problem could be solved by jailing 3,000 thugs, any of whom has a rap sheet long enough to roll all the weed at a Phish concert. Finding, arresting and incarcerating these repeat reprobates could be accomplished with modest budget increases for cops, jails and prisons and without building a single database or registering a single gun.

Which is the real problem. This perspective does not help the gun control industry's end goal.

Despite such weak associations between gun control and crime control, all major gun lobbies ferociously chant the need for licensing and registration. Despite the dismal failure of both processes, despite public distain for more government intrusion, despite gun control industry ranting increasing the probability of their leaders being committed to an asylum or public office, gun control lobbyists endlessly insist that these policies be enacted. It is their mantra, their creed, their inimical ideology. It is a lie poured as the foundation of their next lie:

**The Lie of False Intents:** Proclaiming a false goal to mask one's real objective.

Utterances in unguarded moments are compelling. Bill Clinton once let slip, "Only the police should have handguns." A flyer printed by The Coalition to Stop Gun Violence (originally called "National Council to Control Handguns") pronounced, "It is our aim to ban the manufacture and sale of handguns to private individuals." Dianne Feinstein opined that "Banning guns addresses a fundamental right of all Americans to feel safe." Josh Sugarmann of the Violence Policy Center announced that "...any rational regulator with that authority would ban handguns." Pete Stark – the California Representative to Congress best known for accusing a sitting president of finding amusement in U.S. soldiers' heads being blown off – mumbled, "If a bill to ban handguns came to the house floor, I would vote for it." The Violence Policy Center said "[We are] ... seeking a ban on handgun production." Senator John Chafee declared, "I shortly will introduce legislation banning the sale, manufacture or possession of handguns."

Herein we see a recurring theme more substantial than Michael Moore's intestinal tract and one that traffics the same substance. The end game for the gun control lobby is banning private firearm ownership. Yet doing so is highly problematic. In a land where almost half of households own a firearm – and the other half benefits from the "uncertainty principle" deterrence presented to outlaws who cannot know in advance which of any two households is armed – banning guns is, at best, impossible. Sarah Brady's bootlickers cannot achieve their objectives by slowing or stopping production and sale of firearms, for there would still be millions of guns in circulation ... and in hiding. For a gun ban to succeed there must be gun confiscation, and for confiscation to succeed you must know who has the guns. Ipso facto no registration, no confiscation, no domination.

Lying is a bit like homicide: The first time is gut wrenching, the second time is significantly easier. Call it desensitizing, self-suppression of ethical behavior, or even expanding psychosis. Once the Lie of False Intents was fully exercised, no deception became too flagrant in the pursuit of registration. False intent was intrinsic to selling the Brady Bunch's final solution.

As the registration clarion sounded from the Bradys' Washington, D.C. offices, the armed faction of the American public reacted negatively and the gun control industry responded with balderdash that left even their backers voiceless with disbelief. When gun owners said, "Registration will lead to confiscation," the Bradys et al replied, "No it won't."

If you ever wonder what Simon and Garfunkel were yammering about while euphoniously eliminating the *Sounds of Silence*, you experienced it after this latest lie. An entire nation, regardless of individual political bent, stood in stunned speechlessness, marveling at a combined audacity and legerdemain unknown outside of Goebbels' brainstorming sessions. Even New York Times reporters – having some insight into history and a thread of remaining credibility – didn't buy that one. They recognized:

### The Lie of Historical Obfuscation:
Obscuring or marginalizing historical trends in order to lure people toward the same end.

Firearm registration has been practiced in every oppressed region of the planet from Beijing to Moscow to Washington, D.C. In *every* instance, some or all firearms registered have later been banned and confiscated, or if not confiscated, then regulated into uselessness. Sometimes it happens slowly as it did in Guatemala. Sometimes it is swift as it was in Hitler's Germany. Most often it happens with incremental regulatory sleight of hand as it did in America's Calcutta, New York.

In the late 1960s the city of New York mandated that citizens register their long guns (for urban readers these would be rifles and shotguns). This enactment was in an era where teenagers would carry rifles on the subway en route to firing ranges maintained by their schools. Theodore Weiss, a bespeckled Hungarian immigrant and New York City Council member, proposed licensing long guns for a measly $3/year while proffering elaborate promises that the fee would never increase (today, with associated charges, it hovers around $100). Weiss, Mayor John Lindsey, or anyone who required voter approval for reelection claimed that gun confiscation was not part of the plan. Even the New York Times, whose editorial staff spews passionate prose over every modern gun control measure, demurred by saying that the bill "would protect the constitutional rights of owners and buyers. The purpose of registration would not be to prohibit but to control dangerous weapons."

Fast forward to 1991 New York. Infested by a flea circus city council, crawling prostrate at the leash of Mayor David Dinkins, the citizenry succumbed to a bill that flatly banned private possession of certain semi-automatic rifles and shotguns that had previously been registered by Big Apple's huddled masses. Within short order, notices were sent to the owners of record, and those who refused to surrender their firearms heard heavy boots kicking down their front doors. On the other coast, California's Attorney General sent notices of confiscation to owners of certain grandfathered long guns that through the inactions and overreactions of bureaucracy, went from being legal to illegal overnight. In both cases what was once a mere possession became a registered item, and later became a former possession. Perhaps the politicians who enacted the laws could not foresee future public trustees abusing the registration system. Perhaps Harry Reid isn't a necrophiliac. The probabilities are equally low.

Which brings us to Michael Beard, the anointed head of the National Coalition to Ban Handguns. In an interesting interlude, Beard contrasted his group's pure focus on banning your bedside blaster with that of Handgun Control, Inc., whose originally stated mission was to ban your bedside blaster. Pete Shields, HCI's chief con artist, had abandoned convincing Americans that confiscation was in the public interest, refocusing on the crime control angle. Shields was, if nothing, uncharacteristically honest when he said, "This is not based on any naive hope that criminals will obey such laws." Beard upped the honesty quotient while hammering other gun control industry members' crime control approach. "Some people in the movement felt Americans were worried about crime, and that was one way to approach the problem. That's the problem when you use public opinion polls to tell you what your position's going to be. And I think a lot of the handgun control movement has looked at whatever's hot at the time and tried to latch onto that ... Ultimately, nothing short of taking the product off the market is really going to have an effect ..."

The gun control industry did not remain oblivious to the insurmountable obstacle which they helped manufacture. History is rife with registration leading to confiscation abroad. In the good ol' U-S-of-A confiscation occurred with equally alarming frequency following the same salving politician promises that it would "never happen here." As the millennial gun control crusade faltered under the weight of its own dissimulations, a prudent public questioned the sincerity and sanity of the gun control industry and its leaders. As one wag warned, "Remember Hitler. Remember Lenin. Remember Feinstein!"

# Chapter 5:  The Science That Got Junked

(how Arthur Kellermanns lie)

It is good that most people are not scientists. If you have ever erred by engaging a scientist in cocktail party conversation, and rapidly thereafter prayed for quick death, imagine a world overpopulated with über geeks.

It is due in part to the numbing depth of knowledge possessed by eggheads that most humans blindly accept whatever conclusions scientists and researchers publish in obscure and lightly circulated journals read only by peers and people fond of boredom. Voters also accept research by topic experts because the typical wage slave is not himself a topic expert outside of baseball stats and American Idol telecasts. Asking the garden variety voter to spelunk into the depths of arcane scholarly literature is as fruitful as asking Larry Flynt to kick his porn habit.

Our collective attention deficit disorder has not gone unnoticed by politicos, specifically those in the gun control industry. Indeed they appear to rely upon less-than-studious voters by promoting, purchasing and even producing "studies" with quality rivaling the average karaoke singer. Taxpayer priorities require that they ingest news and views in the same time span as consuming dinner, which leaves no time for investigation during digestion. Ravenous blog scavengers also fall for the conclusions of select studies when they lack the specific education required to unravel academic works. Even hearty civic-minded citizens are detoured by the professor's acquired gift of turgid prose.

**The Lie of Science:** Using weak or irrelevant studies by topic "experts" to convince people that greater minds have reached a valid conclusion.

People benefit from the advance of science, daily employing miracles ranging from bio-engineered medications to Velcro. Everyone is exposed to the "scientific method" providing we paid any attention to teachers during our hormone-soaked high school years. These factors give scientists personas of hyper-intellectual technologists who accept nothing less than absolute precision in their pursuit of knowledge and truth. Common folk picture researchers as above the human frailties of want, greed and ego. Scientists view themselves in the same light. Jesus would find tough competition for a sainthood title against anyone holding an endowed chair.

And nothing could be further from the truth.

Scientists and researchers are human, despite physical appearances. They suffer the same dispositions and objectives as the ordinary hordes. They are not immune to allowing bias to guide their findings or promote only the hand-selected findings of others. Notoriety, peer status and money influence scientific investigation and reporting, especially within studies examining guns and their control. Take a scholar who hates guns, give him a research grant and without fail you will receive a report with results so predictable that your bookie wouldn't wager against it.

Which brings us to the odd and somewhat pathetic story of Arthur Kellermann and his early redoubtable work titled *Protection or Peril?* Published in 1986 and touted to this day by the gun control lobby, poor Arthur's tome has been the butt of jokes among academics ever since, or at least those who have a sense of humor as well as a PhD. One professorial criminologist uses Kellermann's work as an example to his students of how *not* to perform research. At one time *Protection or Peril?* had an unprecedented two entries at JunkScience.com. Only Arthur and Sarah Brady believed his work ... and Sarah likely had her doubts.

Suspicions aside, Kellermann's findings were published in the *New England Journal of Medicine,* an otherwise reputable rag not prone to overly excessive political punditry outside of the gun control debate. This granted Kellermann some desperately needed gravitas because one conclusion in his work is as credible as Bill Clinton's chastity vow. Kellermann handed gun control crusaders a sound bite that ricochets through media echo chambers 25 years later – that a gun in the home is 43 times more likely to kill a family member than to kill someone in self-defense.

Kellermann's paper is what battlefield commanders call a "target-rich environment." The problem is not in finding an issue with Kellermann's methodology – the problem is whether you have enough time left on this mortal coil to recite them all. Due to the expansive nature of this study's inequities, it makes a useful tool for illustrating the many ways a study resembles a capped landfill – they look attractive and green on the surface, but underneath are festering piles of infected rubbish.

**The Lie of Methodology:** Using inappropriate and misleading research methods to create ill-founded conclusions.

The first pothole in Kellermann's road to gun control ruin is that he tallied only dead people. As important as their condition was to the deceased, Kellermann failed to consider the implication of survivors – people who had firearms in the home and used them to dissuade attackers without actually eradicating the marauder. It isn't necessary to dispatch a rapist to Hades – simply poking a snub-nose revolver up his nostril will redirect his inappropriate aspirations. In recent times there were slightly more than 400,000 instances of firearm crimes but nearly 2,500,000 instances of defensive firearm use. In other words the good guys are out-gunning the bad guys by more than 6 to 1. Since many of these armed but non-fatal incidents would have otherwise ended the life of the gun owner, Kellermann's lack of accounting for non-dead homeowners is a rhetorical rut slightly wider than Al Gore's ego, which is now measured in parsecs.

Nor was there adequate advertisement that 85% of Kellermann's reported deaths were suicides. The gun control industry is loath to mention suicides because self-assassination constitutes more than half of all firearm deaths. When this datum is disclosed, the fright value of annual body counts is diminished. It is difficult to stampede voters when slaughter is self-inflicted. For the few gun deaths that were not self-induced in Kellermann's study, little effort was made to illuminate who the killer was and why homicide was the chosen dispute-resolution procedure. If the shooter and shootee were crack house roommates, that might have a bearing on intentional homicides as well as a handful of "accidental" shootings Kellermann recorded. Deadly things occur with the incautious lifestyles of crack heads and other members of the Washington D.C. city government.

**The Lie of Incomplete Comparisons:** Examining only one aspect of a cause-and-effect relationship to create the impression of a single cause and effect.

Kellermann's study – which was restricted to the oddly narrow geography of King County, Washington – also avoided proffering perspective by contrasting gun deaths with non-gun deaths. Doing so would have shown that cruel and stupid people are just as cruel and stupid without a gun or Air Force One. A quick check of King County violent deaths instigated without guns showed roughly the same ratios of homicides, suicides and justifiable killings among both the armed and unarmed populations. Knowing both cause and effect is important in making policy, which is why it is shunned by the gun control industry. Indeed, criminologists have shown that a disproportionate number of violent deaths occur at homes inhabited by people with reckless behaviors such as drinking, drug use and driving across Chappaquiddick bridges.

Another Kellermann statistical oversight was that he didn't account for which gun was used in any of the deaths. Was it the firearm owned by the person residing in the home or a person who got their crack and welfare check at a different address? Instances where an armed thug entered an armed household, and where the resident could not retrieve their firearm were entered into the high side of Kellermann's 43:1 ratio. This methodological quirk was not widely broadcast by the gun control industry, to nobody's surprise.

Yet thirty years and a thousand published critiques later, this "43 times" turpitude reverberates in the endless echo chamber of media and mediocrity. The 2007 Violence Policy Center web site notes that there are "43 deaths for every self-defense homicide."

**The Lie of Inappropriate Experts:**
Using otherwise credible people without subject matter expertise to research or opine on a topic.

What are we then to make of Arthur Kellermann? Why would a criminologist proffer such delinquent research? For openers, Kellermann is not a criminologist. He is a doctor with a Masters of Public Health, which normally earns one a small but steady income at taxpayer expense, free coffee in the faculty lounge and exclusion from most cocktail parties. Kellermann became a star doctor within the seemingly perpetual experiment of integrating epidemiology and gun control public policy. This fad attempts to declare guns – inherently inorganic objects – as an epidemic and thus treatable as a disease. This logical disconnect was more than even intoxicated reporters could tolerate given the self-evident reality that viruses operate on their own in the same way that guns don't. Criminologists, who were angry about not being invited to cocktail parties either, vented their wrath when medical practitioners started muscling in on their turf. Studying infectious bacteria may prepare one for understanding politicians and other parasites, but it does not grant modern shamans with the rigors of sound criminological methodologies. In an ironic twist, working criminologists proceeded to dissect the medical men's gun control studies, diagnosing the weakness of the research and causing many people to wonder if visiting their local pill pusher was healthy.

Is Kellermann stupid? This is doubtful. While being interviewed by the San Francisco Examiner, Kellermann clearly stated the value proposition of firearms by saying, "If that were my wife, would I want her to have a .38 special in her hand? Yeah."

Credibility once had value in most political lies, and especially in the Lie of Science. However, decades of debunking Kellermann-like research – be it in medical criminology or climatology – has started to erode public confidence in the veracity of scientists. Often the theorists themselves are at fault, creating questionable reports while pining for publication and profit. More often it is the propagandist who accelerates public cynicism by misusing studies be they of high or low quality. The gun control industry made Kellermann and his cohorts look far worse than they made themselves appear otherwise, which was a significant achievement on its own.

In fairness to Kellermann, *Protection or Peril?* did disclose that suicides were a major part of King County's total bullet-induced bloodshed. Over nearly thirty years following publication one would have been hard pressed to discover this given how the gun control lobby lobbed the "43 times" rhetorical grenade into the air. Their goal in this inappropriate broadcast was transparent, calculated to convince yet-to-be-armed households that owning a gun was inherently deadly, and through attrition reduce the number of gun owners. Suicides, drug homicides, drunken accidents and even honorable self-defense shootings were nary mentioned, and with good reason.

### The Lie of Picked Cherries: Using selected studies, or selected parts of studies, to substantiate an invalid conclusion.

The Lie of Picked Cherries is the academic twin of the Lie of Context. The first variation on the Lie of Picked Cherries is where only selected studies are referenced. If one academic honestly purports that guns increase crime and another purports that they deter crime, the gun control lobby will select only one of the two. Curiously, pro-gun factions must reference both – to detract from the former and promote the latter – and thus tend to be more forthcoming. Sarah Brady lacks that burden.

The second variation of the Lie of Picked Cherries is slightly less creepy than Barbara Boxer's smile. It involves citing selected parts of a research report as if they were a final conclusion. This is akin to a used car salesman hyping new paint and tires while hiding a firebombed interior and dead hookers in the trunk. This is the gun control lobby's preferred variation of the Lie of Picked Cherries because it has the twin advantages of creating serviceable sound bites and making it difficult to rapidly excavate the whole truth. Often these passages are deeply buried in voluminous reports of bloated prose relating arcane and data-dense details of obscure knowledge. Jacques Cousteau couldn't dive deeply enough to uncover some of these fragments. Yet because they appear in the report, they can be repeated by Josh Sugarmann with what he passes off as a straight face.

It is the *sound bite* that is all important. Concepts that are small, repeatable and poignant travel far and fast. Make them fit the biases of one or another group, and they are transmitted instantly ... almost telepathically. Sometimes they propagate too fast. Truth, however, eventually dons its running shoes and catches up.

Just ask Michael Bellesiles, a man facts caught up to and beat to an academic pulp.

Bellesiles was (*was* being the instructive verb) a professor at Emory University, the same institution where, ironically, Kellermann parked his professorial rump for many years. Bellesiles was a historian who published a book maintaining that firearm ownership in colonial America was relatively rare, a claim opposing all conventional wisdom, common sense and nearly every piece of literature from the period. Through years of research, digging into dusty probate records and other indirect indicators, Bellesiles determined that guns were not widely owned, held mainly by the wealthy colonists, and that the little insurrection called the American Revolution would have been impossible without government subsidies. Bellesiles summarized that "the majority of American men did not care about guns. They were indifferent to owning guns, and they had no apparent interest in learning how to use them."

These conclusions were valuable to the gun control movement in America. For years anti-gun forces had insisted that the Second Amendment protected the rights of the newly formed states to arm militias, and not for individuals to own firearms. In the face of a new and thriving Second Amendment-focused constitutional law cottage industry that was going against this notion, Bellesiles book was a welcome counterpoint – Bellesiles was the gun control movement's Moses, parting the constitutional law Red Sea, leading to the gun-free promised land. Every gun control outfit suffered when speaking against the written will of the people as documented in the Second Amendment. Now the anti-ammo crowd had ammunition – a book that substantiated the argument that "the right of the people to keep and bear arms" could not have possibly meant the right of the people at all.

If this conclusion sounds insane to you, imagine with what Sarah Brady's therapist has to contend.

But Bellesiles' book was buncombe, and watching its dismemberment was like watching an automobile accident in slow motion. An online forum of constitutional scholars and historians, hosted by the UCLA Law School, was the initial point of impact. When Bellesiles' *Arming America* was released to the orgasmic howling of the New York Times, the virtually assembled academics responded in the calm, sedate and boring manner to which they are trained and which keeps them from being invited to cocktail parties. One member of this panel posted a blurb about Bellesiles' tome, to which the universal response was, "That is interesting. I look forward to reading his book." Such high-minded and civil discourse was as short lived as an Obama "you get to keep your medical plan" pledge.

Within days, the first academic reaction crawled across the ether. One scholar wrote (and I paraphrase), "Interesting research, but on page xxx Bellesiles cites a document incorrectly. I suspect he merely mistyped the text, but it does change the meaning. Oh well." Within an hour another professor wrote, "Well, on page yyy he cites a document that I have a copy of, and he got the last bit completely wrong. Maybe he was working from a later version of the law, but he cited the older one. Kinda sloppy." Then all hell broke lose when a few minutes after that, yet another ivy-covered wonk wrote, "You think *that's* bad, look at page zzz! Where did he think up this [expletive expunged]."

From there it devolved from academic dismemberment to a metaphorical lynching. Those who had access to the same data as Bellesiles were finding numerous irregularities. Suspicions were raised when Bellesiles was questioned and reported that much of his recorded data and notes were unavailable, having allegedly been wiped away in a campus flood. Probate records that Bellesiles claimed he had found in San Francisco Superior Court had been incinerated in the 1906 earthquake, and when he revised his claim that the records were actually to be had at the nearby California History Center, that organization noted that Bellesiles never signed their requisite visitor log. It seemed that a historian could not turn a page in *Arming America* without stripping Bellesiles bare, a mental image sure to eliminate hopes of him ever again being invited to any cocktail party.

Academic infighting over Bellesiles' indiscretions occurred behind the scenes. In the public spotlight, Bellesiles was celebrated by the media, fêted in Washington D.C., and awarded the formerly prestigious Bancroft Award. Editorial boards gushed over the conclusions and the New York Times drafted fellow historian Garry Wills to review the Bellesiles book and mock gun owners, writing about a citizen's gun: "Without it, they would not be the self-sufficient persons they consider themselves." The anti-gun lobby and much of the mainly misinformed media twirled about one another, and about Bellesiles in an unseemly embrace heretofore seen only in prison cells. The Second Amendment Antichrist had come, and the demons were dancing.

Had the gun control industry invited contrarian academics to their cocktail party, and gotten them liquored up to the point of imbecility (achieved when they start hitting on Nancy Pelosi), Bellesiles might be coasting to this day on reputation, awards and a publishing career. But he never anticipated the all-too-sober UCLA constitutional law forum mavens, and he never anticipated Clayton Cramer.

Despite having an MA in history – and a passion for early American firearm history at that – Cramer was not at the time a practicing academic, employed instead more profitably as a computer guru. Yet he was one of the historians who kept tripping over factual errors in *Arming America*, and he soon started to compile a list. Cramer became the oracle for critiques on Bellesiles' book (the terminal edition of his list is more than 300 pages, which gives an idea of how many errors there were to expose). The more Bellesiles rose in mainstream esteem, the more academics like Cramer shared exceptions among themselves and tattled to the media about deficiencies within Bellesiles' bestseller. The only non-aligned organization that took notice was C-SPAN. In a surreal moment of television history, they broadcast Bellesiles receiving his Bancroft Award amidst a rostrum of soigné celebrity, followed by the stark image of Cramer alone, armed with a flip chart and a pointer, listing Bellesiles offenses to intellectual fidelity.[1]

At least Bellesiles got some cocktails that night.

Yet people who favor gun control held on to Bellesiles until the bitter end. While being subjected to academic review and tribunal, in fact right through his final banishment from Emory, Bellesiles remained propped up by those propping up the Lie of Picked Cherries. Only when the axe fell on his academic career did mentions of his name disappear from gun control web sites. Upon conviction, even Garry Wills wrote, "I was took. The book is a fraud." The last holdout was the Ninth Circuit Court of Appeals, an outfit known primarily for being overturned by the Supreme Court more often than all other lower courts, possibly combined. Their Judge Reinhardt used *Arming America* in an intellectually chaotic decision arguing that the "right of the people to keep and bear arms" didn't include people. Justice Reinhardt did this not knowing, or given his evident Alzheimer onset, not remembering that Bellesiles had been shamed, his books recalled from the

---

[1] For anyone interested in an accurate telling of colonial guns and ownership, invest in a copy of Clayton Cramer's *Armed America: The Remarkable Story of How and Why Guns Became as American as Apple Pie*

shelves, and his Bancroft Award rescinded. In an act absurd even by the standards of the Ninth "Circus" Court, the decision was pulled from their web site and rewritten, redacting references to *Arming America* – which had earlier been considered evidence.

This is why judges are rarely invited around for cocktails either.

Individual miscreants can change the scope of a debate, but in the age of the Internet where every public utterance is dissected, lone assailants of the truth do not last for long. Though Kellermann's "43 times" triviality has had an exceptionally long shelf life, it too has slowly sunk into disuse as gun control opponents perpetually bash the findings and metaphorically bash Kellermann. To create momentum, lobbying collectives must apply constant pressure and by doing so make the public believe that there is a persistent and growing problem. After all, if Brian Williams can stare unblinkingly at you every night, channeling whatever clandestine teleprompter fodder Sarah Brady has fed NBC, fatigued post-commute characters are bound to believe such buncombe after a bit.

Enter from political stage left the Joyce Foundation. A sedate society founded on the deforestation industry, the Joyces have a peculiar fixation on guns not seen outside of National Guard armories. For the better part of twenty years this foundation puttered along worrying their collective little heads over matters of "religious, charitable, scientific, literary and educational purposes." But after the founder passed on, and the helm of the $100M organization was handed over to Charles U. Daly – a former Congressional Liaison for President Kennedy, and for whom the assassination was likely a Feinsteinesque trauma – the Joyces began redirecting more money into the voracious jowls of the "gun epidemic" research monster. For years the Joyce Foundation has purchased research that attempted to tie medicine, to guns, to public policy through a grant base exceeding $26,000,000. Their unsubtle dodge was to make gun control actionable as a public health issue. Through a fecund flurry of doctored research, they presented to a cringing public the illusion that if unchecked, gun deaths would spread virus-like throughout the world and consume mankind as a mighty plague.

> **The Lie of Mass(ive) Assault:** Generating a huge amount of convincing but inadequate "research" in order to make an issue appear to have "scientific consensus."

Joyce Foundation research tentacles stretch well beyond their Great Lakes base (though they do favor the once respectable Johns Hopkins University and University of California at Davis). Joyce-financed creative criminological studies are performed by physicians and Joyce has endowed the Hopkins Center for Gun Policy and Research as well as the UC Davis School of Medicine and their dodgy docs. Joyce largess went further, bankrolling hyperactive gun control organizations (VPC $700,000; Legal Community Against Violence $400,000) and even the pet projects of wayward politicians (Michael Bloomberg's Mayors Fund to Advance New York City, $175K). They are not shy about their mission to promote gun control policy through all means necessary, coming enticingly close to challenging their 501(c) tax exempt status, proving yet again that zealots tend to do more harm to themselves and their causes than they do to others.

A peculiar method to madness surfaces in medical professionals delving into the muck of homicides. Respected as they are in their fields, their expertise as biological scientists cannot be supplanted into criminological case work. This is akin to trusting an otherwise competent plumber to perform your vasectomy on the theory that pipes are pipes.

## The Lie of Universal Competence:
Using experts in one field of study to opine in a different field, and having their credibility conceal poor research.

Though men and women of medicine are well educated and smarter than the entire congressional brain trust, they are not universal experts. Years of studying hemorrhoids and toe fungus do not prepare one for multivariate statistical analysis of cross-regional and time-ordered homicide trends. Most statisticians live for such rigors and are quirky enough to enjoy crunching massive data sets, which is why they are *never* invited to cocktail parties. Sawbones make weak bean counters. Voters are largely blind to this misguided merging of mastery, in part due to the inherent trust one must put in doctors simply to survive past childhood, but also because the media glosses over the separation of specialists. When a report oozes forth from John Hopkins, top-line conclusions and the name of the institute are reported, but the disconnected wisdom of crime accounting performed by quacks is never contemplated by the press.

One reason people have faith in scientific reporting is a quaint, curious and often corrupt process called "peer review." As the name insinuates, any work of research performed by a person of science is vetted before a panel of peers in the hopes that one or more of them can stay awake long enough to read through bottomless minutia written in prolix prose, and assure before publication that it isn't pure hokum. Those outside of academia view peer review as an iron fence over which all self-respecting researchers must leap, and in front of which hucksters will fall.

Those inside of academia have no such illusions.

## The Lie of Peer Review: Using bands of researchers who share the

same biases to review and approve
suspect research.

Scientists, statisticians and other alleged intellectual purists
are subject to the weaknesses of the flesh, save perhaps alcoholism, but that is mainly due to a lack of exposure via absen-
teeism from the cocktail parties to which they are not invited.
This includes people in medical research. Often they publish
to small journals circulated only to people in their field. Thus
medical researchers at John Hopkins are likely to publish in
journals only read by other medical researchers. If John Hopkins medicos were writing on the pathology of jock itch, their
review peers would have the expertise necessary to catch
stupid mistakes and outright shams. But if the same researcher is publishing statistically heavy criminological investigations, their reviewing peers won't catch what they do not
understand. A case of the bogus leading the blind.

This iniquity has not gone unnoticed by the rest of the research community, medical and medicated alike. Robert
Higgs, a fellow with enough letters after his name to start an
alphabet soup factory, is troubled by the bias-induced weakness of the peer review system. He should know given that he
has endured four decades in academia, during which he has
been a peer reviewer for over thirty professional journals, and
a research proposal reviewer for the National Science Foundation, the National Institutes of Health and a number of
private foundations. "Peer review," he writes, "on which lay
people place great weight, varies from being an important
control, where the editors and the referees are competent and
responsible, to being a complete farce," The main obstacle for
a researcher to get published is to find a journal whose editors
share the researcher's bias. "Any journal editor who desires,
for whatever reason, to reject a submission can easily do so by
choosing referees he knows full well will knock it down;
likewise, he can easily obtain favorable referee reports."

If that doesn't inspire confidence in the scientific peer review process, then sanity persists.

The sorcerers at the Joyce-anointed John Hopkins University can make the process easier by peddling papers to medical journals. By staging crime data in the familiar framework of health care research, and by selecting journals whose mastheads are populated by publishers who editorialize on tragic inner-city emergency room scenes, their work is rarely given the proper scrutiny. Indeed, if the same papers were presented to criminological journals, they would be quickly recognized as crimes in commission, where the perp was armed with a word processer. Criminologists encountering such "medical" research are tempted to call the cops.

This putrid practice has attracted attention of people tangent to fields in question. Gary Mauser is no mental 90-pound weakling, holding a Ph. D. in Psychology, which won't get you a cup of coffee in Texas or an invitation to a cocktail party anywhere. He shares Higgs' concerns, but from the close perspective of being in the medical trade himself. "Medical researchers, no matter how well qualified in their fields, are typically not capable of adequately reviewing papers in criminology. MDs, even when they have been trained in statistics, typically have not been trained in social science research methods nor are they familiar with research on the relevant questions in criminology. Thus, it should come as no surprise when medical journals allow studies to be published that commit elementary statistical errors."

With the Joyce Foundation paving the path to publication, researchers like Arthur Kellermann who on a good day get it wrong, historians like Michael Bellesiles who doctor their data, university factotums faking it, and a peer review process that only P.T. Barnum could appreciate, it is little wonder faith in science, medicine and academia is slipping. One could ask a doctor about this, but they aren't invited to cocktail parties these days.

# Chapter 6: Technologies That Will Never Be
## (how Paul Helmkes lie)

Paul Helmke should play poker. He's got the face for it.

It is not that Helmke's mug has the blandness of a bowl of cold oatmeal (it does). Nor is his face particularly suited for intimidating Texas Hold'em opponents (it isn't). Helmke's face is perfect for poker because it maintains its steady facade even when the most unbelievable and borderline apocalyptic drivel spews forth from its uncontrollable major orifice.

He could be Bill Clinton's stunt double for disclaiming intern interactions.

Within nanoseconds of a mass murder on the Virginia Tech campus, Helmke – the ineffectual front man for the Brady Campaign – managed to shove Chuck Schumer out of television camera range long enough to declare that several forms of failed and untested gun control measures would have prevented the massacre. Paul must have stifled dozens of snickers, for only a poker player *par excellence* could pitch gun control as a cure to mass murder without knowing anything about the assassin, his means, methods, weapons or evidence of a bin Laden family relationship.

Emboldened by ignorance, Helmke asserted in a trifecta of tripe that tragedies like the VA Tech bloodbath could be prevented by Brady Bill background checks (the shooter passed all background checks) or reinstituting Dianne Feinstein's "assault weapon" ban (the shooter used two standard capacity handguns and grandfathered pre-ban accessories). Still wearing a face that Wild Bill Hickok couldn't read, Helmke howled that within the two-hour lapse between Seung-Hui Cho's slaughters and suicide, "New technologies, such as microstamping and other ballistic identification systems, might have allowed authorities to identify the Virginia Tech shooter earlier, before his second, most deadly, rampage."

Helmke went all in and criminologists called his bluff.

## **The Lie of Technology:** Asserting that one or another technology will correct a perceived social disorder.

Arthur Clarke wasn't kidding when he said, "Any sufficiently advanced technology is indistinguishable from magic." Ignite a palm full of flash powder in front of a band of aborigines and the tribe will elect you as their next shaman. In the digital age the average voter has little knowledge of how Google works, making it one small step away from being Internet magic. When Helmke's missionaries hold forth technologies combining ballistics, micro-engraving and computers, less worldly members of the American tribe see miracles in the making.

All snake oil is sold that way.

The notion of being able to identify firearms used in crimes via residual forensic evidence has long been a law enforcement daydream. Rudimentary matching of recovered slugs can tie a firearm to a crime – providing the used bullets came from the same box of ammo and are obtained from different crime scenes in reasonably close chronological order. Helmke's hordes combine this staple of television crime dramas with the nearly omniscient results of Google's databases to create post-modern political flash powder. Helmke vowed that if every firearm in America had its ballistic baseline logged into a massive government data warehouse, then any firearm felony could be solved with the criminological equivalent of scanning YouTube videos.

Paul Helmke hasn't been to Home Depot lately.

Buried in the bowels of every Home Depot is a Ballistic Tracing Recalibration tool. It is an ingenious piece of technology, simple in its approach and devastatingly good at permanently altering the ballistic "fingerprint" of any firearm. It takes almost no talent or understanding of firearm technology to use – any street thug could make their firearm completely untraceable. The operation takes less than sixty seconds, and worst yet the Ballistic Tracing Recalibration costs a mere $3$^{95}$.

Don't look for "Ballistic Tracing Recalibration" in the Home Depot catalog. Look instead for "needle file."

Popular with machinists since the Iron Age, needle files have been endlessly used to shave metal from the inside of castings, including mass-manufactured firearm parts. Gunsmiths routinely employ needle files to hone barrels, bushings and other ballistic touch points. This is where Home Depot's Ballistic Tracing Recalibration tool provides value to perps. Any surface over which soft bullet lead speeds leaves lasting impressions in the slug, with telltale grooves being the most noticeable markings. Firing pins create somewhat less unique impressions on spent cartridges. These gouges and dents are what Paul Helmke wants to catalog at the moment of manufacture of every handgun, along with the serial number of the firearm and the buyer's Social Security number plus DNA and urine specimens.

Like serial numbers on the sides of crime guns, bullet-touching firearm parts will be whittled away by enterprising drug runners, mugging specialists and Robert Blake. If you see a number of sinister-looking but unelected characters lurking on aisle 16 at your local Home Deport, then you know where to find needle files. Unless these suspicious folk are examining metal pipes, in which case it is the William Ayers chapter of the Obama reelection committee.

**The Lie of Snowflakes:** Claiming that every unit of a mass manufactured product is inherently unique and will always remain that way.

The fundamental flaw of gun tracing systems is the immediately invalid assumption that every firearm is unique or can be made such. As Henry Ford proved, the primary benefit of assembly line manufacturing is that removing all variation from unit to unit creates more products with less cost. Complex machines need to be nearly identical and parts completely interchangeable, be they carburetors, firing pins or Chicago politicians. The side effect of producing identical parts for identical guns is that you get nearly identical ballistics. Over time and usage a firearm *may* develop its own characteristic through use, misuse, abuse and varying quantities of applied gun powder. But at their moment of birth and proposed "fingerprinting," two handguns are more similar than fraternal twins, the primary difference between twin guns and twin humans being that at age two the children are vastly more destructive.

Identical components not only allow for mass manufacturing, they also enable enormous aftermarkets for replacement and custom parts which change a gun's "fingerprints" more rapidly than a belt sander could change yours. Are you unhappy with the performance of the original barrel in your model 1911 (the official sidearm of the U.S. military from … well … 1911 through 1985, and the most copied handgun on the planet)? Then buy a new barrel and in the process alter the ballistic "fingerprint" with which your piece was born. The same applies for the firing pin, extractor, port or any other part that might touch the bullet or case.

Google reports 21,200 pages where you can obtain a replacement barrel for your 1911. It is worth noting that many of the returned Google results are incorrect, as are most of the matches from ballistic databases.

These issues are not unknown to Helmke or his disciples of disinformation. The National Research Council reported that "ballistic fingerprinting" technology wasn't capable. The Bureau of Forensic Services – located deep within the entrails of California's Department of Justice – said that markings on bullets were not "permanently defined like fingerprints or DNA." The Handbook of Firearms and Ballistics noted that the same gun will produce different markings on bullets and casings, and different guns can produce similar markings. Maryland has tracked ballistics since the year 2000 and their top cops report that a single solitary crime was solved with the data. You would find more positive matches conducting HIV tests in a convent.

Yet Helmke's poker face remains unchanged.

Aside from apparent pharmaceutical abuse, why would Paul Helmke continue his campaign for universal ballistic fingerprinting when the technology is congenitally defective? He does so not out of delusion (though his delusional status has yet to be debunked) but because of the intended side effect of cataloging every firearm made or imported. A database of ballistics is futile, but provides false justification to record to whom a gun was sold or traded. Helmke's "fingerprinting" creates de facto registration. Yes, registration – that "common sense" legislation Hilary Clinton peddled the same year Maryland instituted its demonstrably useless ballistic fingerprinting program and two years after hubby Bill's demonstrably useless fidelity vows were Lewinskied.

No wonder Sarah Brady hired Helmke. She doesn't have his poker face.

**Lie of Concealment:** Promoting a seemingly benign policy to surreptitiously enact a malignant one.

A major missing piece of Helmke's registration puzzle is the handgun stockpile already in private ownership. In the year that Hillary stumped for registration regimes, there were around 65,000,000 handguns owned by citizens, which was roughly 99 times more than were manufactured for sale in the U.S. that same year. Firearms have amazing longevity and thus over the years America has assembled a handy private armory. Helmke and Clinton's gun registration ruse could only succeed if every civic-minded gun-owning adult – upwards of 100 million of them – toted pistols into their local sheriff's office, and paid to have them ballistically mapped and registered under their name. Each cop shop would have to employ a specialist trained in one of several possibly incompatible systems for taking the ballistic "fingerprint." Some legislative proposals have required the registration process to be repeated every year just in case you bought a replacement barrel or shot enough burglars to alter the scarring your gun makes on slugs.

Imagine a nationwide Department of Motor Vehicles without the ambiance, efficiency or charm.

What makes the gun control industry's proposals tactically problematic it is that there might be a tiny bit of resistance to registering currently owned and unregistered firearms. If non-registration rates in Canada are any indication, Americans would ignore such mandates as thoroughly as they do their diets, knowing full well that what the government doesn't (yet) know can't keep poor bureaucrats up at night. Genetic American resistance to being tagged and tracked creates insurmountable barriers to Helmke's backdoor registration initiative, which is why the gun control industry opted to "fingerprint" only new handguns. To the average gun owner – who in any given year is unlikely to be in the market for a new firearm – such a scheme might be painless enough to accept. Thus, registration through ballistic fingerprinting is designed to start as a pleasant engagement, in much the same way as date rape.

> **The Lie of Increments:** Claiming that only a small intrusion into private matters is planned, knowing it can be made infinitely more intrusive later.

Only bad ideas vie with firearms for mechanical longevity. When uniformly negative assessments of ballistic fingerprinting doomed Helmke's original designs, new technological nostrums were instantly brewed. One abstruse alternative had a more diabolical destination than mere registration. It sought to make the manufacture of firearms cost prohibitive and thus place self-protection out of the economic reach of anyone with less wealth than the House of Saud. The new scheme dictated gun and ammo manufacturers imprint unique marks on casings or bullets. Such requirements would add hundreds of dollars to the price of a handgun, geometrically multiply the price of a box of ammo, require that every bullet be registered, and necessitate renting your kids out for medical experiments to pay for an hour at the shooting range.

In other words, it was a larger, fresher and more fragrant pile of manure.

> **The Lie of Even Better Technology:** Insisting that failed technologies will or have improved while ignoring the inherent problem.

A myriad of proposals fall under the enormous umbrella called "microstamping." One technology entails using individually marked firing pins in each newly manufactured gun. Firing pins are slender rods that at high velocities slam into cartridges in order to ignite gunpowder. This allegedly leaves a matching imprint on the spent cartridge that for a single type of handgun (center fire automatics) is automatically deposited at the crime scene (revolvers and rimfire handguns either leave no case or do not use an engravable firing pin, which means huge numbers of popular guns leave no marked cases at all – thus these popular guns would eventually to be banned since they would be "untraceable"). The tips of firing pins are a fraction of an inch in width and microstamps are a few microns tall – slightly larger than Michael Moore's sexual charisma.

Microscopically engraved firing pins are perfect candidates for the Ballistic Tracing Recalibration tool.

Unfortunately for Home Depot, needle files are unnecessary for altering microstamped firing pins – they tend to do it themselves in short order. The concussive force inside of handguns – 1,500 foot pounds of energy on the high end – is rough on many components. Even the relatively modest force applied to firing pins is sufficient to eradicate microstamped etchings so small that within their groves you could hide Richard Daley's soul. A publication by the U.S. government agency responsible for enforcing firearm laws noted that firing pins can readily be swapped (damn you Henry Ford!) and the impressions made by microstamping technology wear away after as few as ten rounds are fired from the gun.

Ten rounds is about 1/1000th of the number discharged per second during a Dirty Harry movie.

Sensing that easily exchangeable internal components like firing pins might be problematic to pitching new firearm registration programs, some members of the gun control industry looked down the other end of the technical barrel. If guns themselves could not be made exorbitantly expensive and automatically registerable, then ammunition might. Few people have rational reasons to disassemble commercially manufactured bullets or have their components parts replaced. Mandating that every slug or case be uniquely marked, and that citizens register every bullet with the government would achieve the occasionally stated goal of the gun control industry, namely keeping you from owning any.

If nothing else, Helmke's Huns can be praised for their consistency in missing the perfectly obvious. Like an over-aged prostitute who still walks streets every night, they fail to understand that what they offer is unappetizing. Visibly obvious legislative flaws cause voters to say "no thank you" while suppressing the urge to regurge.

Such is the case with bullet serialization. Helmke stuffed his sagging sacks of microstamping technology into the new brazier of engraved brass. The theory was that ammunition manufacturers could easily retool their factories, installing high speed lasers (that did not exist) to uniquely mark every bullet in a box. Helmke's associates in the gun control industry extracted cost estimates from their lower-most orifice, telling the public that the price of recreational ammo would rise mere pennies. Their cost estimates were held with some minor suspicion given that nobody in the Brady Campaign, Violence Policy Center or other intellectual brothels had ever been in the ammunition manufacturing business.

**The Lie of Business Acumen:** Making inaccurate claims about the limited impact to business and customers in order make a costly proposal sound reasonable.

People in the bullet business pointed out the combined effects of the non-existent technologies and the slowing of a otherwise rapid process (over 10 billion rounds served ... each year) would raise the price of a 50 round box of ammo to about $200, or an eleven-fold increase. Given that shooting enthusiasts can easily expend 500 rounds of ammo in an afternoon, bullet serialization becomes expensive even by congressional standards.

Which was the plan.

Cost aside, there was also the pesky issue of having lasers powerful enough to rapidly engrave brass in the same room as several tons of gun powder, an oversight that even caught the interest of the Occupational Health and Safety Administration. It simply would not do having a factory full of workers blown directly up to heaven if someone failed to recalibrate the engraving laser one morning.

Yet Helmke's mug stayed perfectly unperturbed.

Inconveniences like exploding employees slowed the progress of legislation long enough for cops to question some other aspects of bullet serialization. Most recreational shooters tend to leave their empty, spent cases on the ground. What would stop a smarter than average criminal – say a Rahm Emanuel – from scooping up a double handful of used brass to scatter at his next crime scene? Most guns used in crimes are stolen, as is a fair amount of ammo. Serialized bullets, traceable only to the original buyer, create an incredible onus on everyone aside from the ne'er do wells who stole the ammo. Whenever the thief or his criminal customers fired a stolen round, the cops would visit the person who legally purchased the ammo, forcing the citizen to dig out the same police theft report every time. Lots of police time. Lots of your time. No time behind bars for the criminals. Gun enthusiasts well acquainted with home-loaded ammo noted that the business of hand-manufacturing rounds would likely blossom before the ban as thugs formerly content with swiping bullets would start building them in bulk.

Still, every muscle on Helmke's mug stayed steady.

Helmke had an ace in his hole. He possessed the Holy Grail of Gun Control. Helmke had at the ready a technological end-all for preventing firearm misuse by criminals, small children and Rambo. Helmke possessed a debate-ending device that did not involve fragile firing pin engravings or immolating employees at ammunition factories. Helmke had the Smart Gun!

He even kept a straight face during a "smart" gun press conference.

Helmke and his handlers' idea is to make inanimate objects intelligent. Though the very concept has been disproven by sixty years of television, great sums of cash have been spent by the gun control industry to promote the idea, and some spare change was tossed to the New Jersey Institute of Technology in an attempt to invent the technology. The simplistic concept is to make the firearm aware of who is pulling the trigger and to not fire if the user was unknown to the gun. This way a stolen gun supposedly could not be fired by a crook and a kid couldn't accidentally discharge a round into the babysitter.

If you catch your kids surfing porn after they disabled the nanny filters on your home computer, the inviability of "smart guns" becomes self-evident.

Most "smart gun" technology involves identifying the user via matching accessories – such as an encoded bracelet – or by measuring the shooter's hand size, relative grip strength and degree of halitosis (scientists are still working on the problem of one's "morning breath" disabling the firearm). The gun would be programmed to recognize bracelets belonging to people allowed to use a gun, providing of course that gun owners are wearing their bracelet at the time they need to fire. After all, not everything accessorizes with every outfit, and having to detour naked from the shower to the jewelry box before blasting a burglar exposes you in multiple ways.

"Smart gun" technologies were even evaluated by the federal government within the caverns of the Sandia National Laboratories. They evaluated various "smart gun" schemes, examining the system's physical characteristics, cost, operation and combat-scenario feng shui. Oddly, situational reliability was not an evaluation criterion, though police surveyed in the same report said that reliability was nearly three times more important than the next issue on the list. Radio frequencies were intrinsic to the top four alternatives in Sandia's 1996 report, an era before mass implementation of cell phones, home wi-fi, ubiquitous cordless telephones and enough wireless toys that your kid's college fund was likely blown on batteries. The outcome of life-and-death situations should not depend on how chatty your teenage daughter is.

These "smart guns" – which are already looking a little dumb – might alternately use Dynamic Grip Recognition whereby your uninjured hand size and strength are measured, making the firearm completely useless in high-stress, fist-clenching situations such as deterring a mugger. In both systems, computer chips in one gizmo or another would perform the analysis and decide if you were indeed authorized to shoot your rapist.

That's if the batteries are fresh.

> **The Lie of Pantyhose:** Claiming that everyone's situations are similar enough that one-size-fits-all solutions work universally.

Consider yourself lucky if you ask any woman about one-size-fits-all pantyhose and get only a nasty look in return. It is the common myth of both the pantyhose and gun control industries that such systems work. But akin to a lanky gal waddling penguin-like down the street, pantyhose crotch panel at her knees, real people facing real self-defense situations have vastly different needs, and those needs are unknown before the event. This reality explains why voters have decided that smart is dumb. "Smart gun" gizmos have been on the market for more than a decade with near zero sales because nobody wants to risk their lives on hardware unintelligent enough to instantly know the emergency situation.

Which explains the name change that Paul Helmke uttered without a twitch of conscience.

In political marketing, words mean everything and change constantly. "Liberal" was once a good word describing a predilection toward freedom. Over time "liberals" started campaigning for wholesale elimination of freedoms including the freedom to own a gun. Likewise, the phrase "smart guns" slowly obtained a negative connotation even among voters with little understanding of firearm technology. The gun control industry is, if nothing else, marketing savvy. Sensing that "smart guns" was a detrimental term, gun prohibition practitioners reclassified them as "personalized guns." This not only avoided the depreciated term, it added a little touch of familiarity. "Personalized guns" sounded a lot like "personal computer," and we all know how much we *love* those. Rumor was that Microsoft once worked on "personalized gun" technologies, but customers didn't like having to reboot their firearms between shots. When a drug-addled ex-husband is breaking down your back door, an 80% solution is not good enough.

Just ask a cop.

Aside from his face, Helmke's other consistency has been excluding police from his mandates, mainly because cops insist. Police – who daily face situations not covered in cadet school – dislike the idea of having guns no smarter than Britney Spears and thus twice as dangerous as Courtney Love. "Smart guns" were once peddled in part to protect law enforcement officers from criminals grabbing their firearms during a struggle. Officers declined to carry such weapons noting that losing a sidearm during a struggle was less likely than a "smart" gun not working. A gun so smart that it doesn't always work would ensure the aforementioned struggle would happen. So for "smart guns," etched ammo, microstamping and all other proposals, Helmke's Hellions exempted police from participating, allowing them instead to acquire untraceable guns and ammo since they were perfectly safe in police hands.

Except when the Wayne, New Jersey Police Department lost three MP5 submachine guns.

Or when a thief stole the Seattle Chief of Police's 9mm Glock from the front seat of a squad car and another thief did the same to a Salem, New Hampshire patrol officer.

Or when one fourth of the shotguns belonging to the Long Beach, California PD went missing.

Or when the Tuxedo Park Police Chief misplaced eight department handguns ... Or when the Salt Lake County Sheriff Office SWAT team left an M4 assault rifle in the road after a stand-off ... Or when the Rockville, Maryland headquarters of the Nuclear Regulatory Commission's office lost 15 out of 17 firearms it once held ... Or an M-16 disappeared from a patrol car in Grand Prairie, Texas ... Or when the Bureau of Alcohol, Tobacco, Firearms and Explosives lost track of 76 weapons, ten of which were "left in a public place" ... Or when several assault rifles were swiped from the truck of a Clayton County patrol car ... Or when an FBI special operations van parked outside a Memphis hotel was looted and a cache of assault rifles, grenade launchers, M-16 military rifles, shotguns and ammunition were swiped ... Or when the FBI misplaced 449 side arms and submachine guns ... Or when the DEA lost 91 weapons ... Or when five separate federal agencies lost about 150,000 weapons, later found on dead people and drug runners ...

Paul Helmke just blinked!

# Chapter 7: Laws That Never Work
(how Janet Renos lie)

"There are only three crimes on the books," a cop acquaintance said over beers. "The crime of thinking wrong, the crime of being stupid and the crime of driving with your head up your ass."

His cynical citation is not without merit. Criminal law – and thus what is deemed as criminal acts – has a narrow function, which is to keep bad people from hurting good people, with only the IRS being immune from this rule. In more advanced societies this principle is stretched like legislative Silly Putty, until the intent of criminal law is an unrecognizable and hideously deformed blob, similar to Barney Frank's post-coital facial expressions (apologies to everyone who suffered that mental image).

Since sparing good people from the skullduggery of bad folk or inattentive idiots is the mission of criminal law, then the number of crimes defined by law should be relatively small. Granted, criminals are clever and constantly inventing new forms of carnage and chaos, much of which is reflected in the federal budget or the ACORN Pimping Agency. However, simpler crimes – such as using guns to rob and kill – present a tiny set of prohibitions. Don't shoot recklessly, don't use guns to rob people and don't murder your neighbor.

In America these three injunctions are codified in over 20,000 laws.

Significant overlap exists within the estimated 20,000 pieces of legislation. Basic prohibitions are repeated across 50 states, 3,140 counties and innumerable cities, towns and socially isolated bergs (hello Two Eggs, Florida). Given the propensity for politicians to pass bad laws as rapidly as prostitutes pass along equally ghastly disorders, the antiquated estimate of 20,000 local, county, state and federal gun control laws is likely low. Their one unifying theme is that by and large none of them have worked.

## The Lie of Legislative Salvation:
Assuring people that law by itself will cure a social ill.

Politicians routinely utter the profligate promise that their legislative prose will put a stop to petty crime, major crime, global climate fluctuation and post-nasal drip. Half hidden behind barricades of microphones, lawmakers announce with great fervor and conviction that a few words scratched upon a piece of paper will instantly halt inhumanity. Politicians palaver the public that new gun control writs send messages that make your neighborhood mugger quake with fear.

"Gun control? It's the best thing you can do for crooks and gangsters," was Sammy "The Bull" Gravano's summary. Sammy should know. He was first order thug within the legendary Gambino crime syndicate. A petty thief by age eight and a made man in his 20s, Sammy earned his criminal keep using violence as his primary differentiator. Those twenty thousand pieces of paper were an aid to Sammy. "I want you to have nothing. If I'm a bad guy, I'm always gonna have a gun. Safety locks? You will pull the trigger with a lock on, and I'll pull the trigger. We'll see who wins."

The congenital weakness of the Lie of Legislative Salvation is that lawbreakers rarely obey laws. Indeed, they would lose rank in the Thugs Union if they obeyed laws. Even lawmakers don't obey laws – Ted Stevens, Rod Blagojevich, Larry Craig, Charlie Rangel … well, the list is rather long and anti-deforestation legislation prohibits full itemization. People – and we will stretch the definition of *people* to included the elected and incarcerated, two groups of interchangeable parts – obey laws to the extent that the price of being prosecuted causes them to recalculate malfeasance's risks and rewards. More people drive above the speed limit than commit armed robbery because the penalty for speeding is low compared to the benefit of getting home quickly, whereas the penalty of prison is high compared to the benefit of whatever petty profits can be lifted from an ATM patron or convenience store cash register.

That is why so many Obama cabinet members cheat on their taxes. The rewards are high and the risk of being tried is south of zero.

Risk/reward analysis occurs to even drug-addled inner-city mobsters. To have any effect, laws protecting people from Crips, Bloods and Congressmen must either reduce the reward obtained from crimes, or amplify the penalty such that no sentient scofflaw would dare violate an ordinance. For gun control laws to work they must target hoodlums who routinely misuse guns. Miscreants must be caught and have the laws enforced upon them.

Which leads us to the Clinton administration and their schizophrenia poster child, Janet Reno. Seriously, have you ever looked at her eyes? There are too many residents in that apartment.

With a press parade surpassed only by coronations and Robert Downey, Jr. rehab admissions, the Clinton administration ushered in the Brady Bill, named after Jim Brady, the patron saint of gun control and other lost causes. The one

Brady Bill objective agreed upon by gun control advocates and detractors was that keeping known criminals from buying firepower was a good idea. Through compromise the National Instant Check System – known as NICS – came to staggering, Frankenstein-like life. The system wired every gun store in the country to an FBI-managed database containing a list of people prohibited from being in the same zip code as a gun. Clinton minions proclaimed that criminals would be nabbed at the point of purchase, and that the full penalty of federal law would send these reprobates (the gun buying felons, not Clinton administration press officers) away for extended stints in penitentiaries, or for extraordinary infractions the White House press office.

Sammy Gravano snickered.

The federal threat was not trivial. Convicted felons – forbidden to own a bullet much less purchase a piece at retail – faced the possibility of ten years of involuntary romantic interchange with a new cell mate in a federal hoosegow. This might suit Barney Frank, but even hardened criminals think twice about being on the receiving end of 3,650 days of prison rape. Making the criminal's risk/reward calculations more compelling is that the federal penal system is rather flexible about where you meet your next lover. A thug and his homeboys may find reasonable comfort and protection in the same slammer, but the feds have an ample transportation budget and can send a felon-in-possession to the other end of the country. Take a Crip from Queens and let him battle it out in Beaumont, Texas with a contingent from MS-13, and the risk side of his mental equation suddenly shifts.

Assuming an arrest is pending.

For all her byzantine bravado and on-camera indignation, Clinton's top cop, Janet Reno, was a little lax on enforcement. Perhaps formulating assault strategies on church compounds and Cuban refugees took most of the copious spare time available to her multiple personalities. Janet's priorities forced her to largely let slide enforcement of federal laws forbidding known felons to purchase firearms. Around 536,000 prohibited buyers were flagged as ineligible by the NICS system during Reno's oversight. No federal marshals swooped down upon them while they were standing in the gun store. Only 6,700 (1%) of these suspects were charged with breaking the law, and that was typically a prosecution under state law by local law enforcement and not Janet Reno 911. About 3,353 prohibited individuals (way less than 1%) managed to obtain firearms anyway, but Reno's Raiders only investigated 110 (3%) of them.

"The goal is to keep guns out of the hands of criminals, it is not designed to be a prosecutorial tool," was what one Reno press parasite said. "Rather, a representative of a state or local criminal justice agency in the state where the firearm transaction is proposed to occur will make this decision ..."

Federal law. Federal background checks. Federal violations. *State* enforcement. Perhaps the 20,000 gun control laws exist in the vague hope that some law enforcement agency at some level of government might accidentally prosecute a criminal.

### The Lie of Accountability: Falsely assuring people that those charged with performing a duty will attempt to do so.

Little wonder that criminals have little respect for the law since laws are the least threatening part of their profession. However, once in a great while law is enforced and criminals respond in ways more predictable than Rahm Emanuel's four letter vocabulary.

Federal gun control history has a meandering past. Central government was silent on the subject until 1934. This was the era of the original American mobster who trafficked Canadian whiskey instead of crack cocaine. Like their modern brethren, the gangsters of old used violence primarily against other mobsters, and occasionally against civilians who were dumb enough to disrupt their business. With business booming and every unemployed strong-arm looking to make a buck in the

Depression, competition was fierce and inter-gang assassinations were frequent, but gun violence against the citizenry was rare. The mob's favorite firearms for eradicating the employees of other gangs were machine guns and sawed-off shotguns.

The feds knew they could not legally outlaw firearms, so they taxed them ... though the government waited until after Prohibition was repealed and the reason for mob gunplay had gone away.

Specific types of firearms favored by the criminals du jour have been perennial targets for the gun control industry. Al Capone was not sufficiently concerned about a stiff tax on Tommy Guns because he didn't even bother to pay income tax. Likewise a ban on Dianne Feinstein's mythical "assault weapons" does not dissuade modern bootleggers because they do not use those firearms, and even if they did, legislative exposition is not terribly deterring to desperados. Neither are the 1938 federal laws against interstate sales of firearms. If you can import a couple of tons of smack and surplus Chinese AK47s from Afghanistan, prohibitions against forwarding them to Fresno are minor details. Such direct dealing also eliminates a fair amount of the firearm sales paperwork mandated in 1968 legislation. When shortchanging your closest business associates results in instant death, writs lack intimidation.

Which tidily brings us back to Janet Reno.

While Janet was reformulating her Waco initiative for a Miami neighborhood, the police department of Richmond, Virginia decided to hijack part of Reno's agency in order to give local felons a reason to find day jobs. Being at interstate highway crossroads – one running up from Janet Reno's home town of Miami, and the other coming from the port city of Norfolk – Richmond was rapidly descending into a violent drug-running way port, earning it one of the highest per capita murder rates in the country. Recreational homicide had risen to where a fresh body appeared every day in a city with fewer than a quarter million survivors. Felons were routinely caught with guns, but the most serious charges local cops could file were for the drugs, not the pistols. Well known and well armed felons were typically back on Richmond streets in less time than it takes to say "habeas your mama's corpus."

City cops began using federal law to slow the carnage and convince local miscreants that holding a gun was a career-limiting strategy. Tag teaming with the U.S. Attorney for eastern Virginia – the same people Reno dissuaded from enforcing federal gun laws – and the Bureau of Alcohol, Tobacco and Firearms, Richmond's constabulary instigated a game of catch, incarcerate and relocate. Richmond police would turn their better-known gangstas over to the Feds if said suspect was a felon found in possession of so much as a bullet. Federal law called for compound sentencing if some combination of criminal activity was included such as possessing drugs and guns, gun possession by a fugitive from another state, holding a gun while under a felony indictment or being at a Chicago Democrat fundraiser. Arrests that previously earned dope runners six-month stints in the county lock-up suddenly loomed as eight to ten years exiled in a federal pen far from home, family, friends, fellow gang members or compatible prison paramours.

They called it Project Exile.

Based on the curious notion that enforcing existing laws and targeting known criminals might reduce crime, the project showed instant progress – the variety or progress with which Janet Reno remains unfamiliar. Seemingly overnight, Richmond's murder rate dropped 41%, all violent crime dipped 22%, and formerly tough thugs would shout, "I don't have a gun!" when a cop asked for their driver's license. Local LEOs heavily advertised Project Exile, reporting when well known gangland operators were sentenced and exiled, each for an average of four and a half years. They advertised on television and in buses. When Richmond cops made the entire city aware that ex-cons with cappers were heading for the cooler, violent crime plunged.

Richmond drug runners showed more intelligence than Janet Reno, which admittedly ranks as a small achievement.

**Lie of Moving Sources:** Changing the claimed source or cause of a perceived problem when facts make it necessary.

Herein lay the primary lie of the gun control industry – that laws work. Sans enforcement, laws are mere suggestions. Speeding on California highways is condoned because highway patrolmen are relatively few in number and too busy scraping lane-splitting motorcyclist off the asphalt. But speed through any small Southern town and a ticket is guaranteed because down-home sheriffs have little else to occupy their time plus a perverse profit motive. Similar speeding laws exist in Los Angeles, California and Laurel, Mississippi, but in Laurel the fine for speeding is crucifixion.

Violent criminals *do* think differently than average citizens, a tidbit the gun control industry ignores out of necessity. Career criminals with violent streaks have a general disregard for everybody. Their moral balance sheet runs deficits that they ignore as completely as Congress ignores the federal variety. Beating, maiming and killing for trivial gains is a perfectly rational notion to this brand of desperado. Acts of violence that would churn your stomach are morning to-do items for your average thug.

Popular in police training is a video confession from a mugger. This enterprising fellow was versed at swiping handbags from retired women in Janet Reno's greater Miami metro area. It was easy work given that the average little old lady has no physical strength compared to the 220-pounder police had in possession and on camera. Earlier that day the mugger had managed to find a feisty old gal who was unwilling to release her purse. The surprised suspect did what any Neanderthal would do. He beat and kicked the woman until she had a broken jaw, several broken ribs, internal bleeding, missing teeth and a near-death experience.

When asked why he felt it necessary to bludgeon an old woman, the culprit replied, "If the damn bitch would have just let go I wouldn't have had to beat her up."

**The Lie of More:** Insisting that more of the same will produce a different outcome.

Common criminals and the gun control industry think alike. End goals are supremely important – all existential realities are secondary. This applies to muggers, mass murderers and MSNBC reporters. Yet the gun control industry and their political allies insist that a society-wide prohibition will change the behavior of the miscreant minority. This theory requires an unsound but seemingly unshakable belief that people who disobey laws as a lifestyle will instantly obey yet another law. Missing from this amoral legislative equation is the impact it has on everyone who has not led a criminal existence ... at least not until new laws arise to forbid you what was once legal, like your bedside revolver.

Welcome to the criminal class. Line on the left, one wrist slap each.

**The Lie of Mass Micro:** Claiming that a law restraining the masses will control the minority who actually cause problems.

Extreme cases of disregard for laws and humanity illustrate the situation with painful clarity. Muggers maiming old ladies to steal Social Insecurity checks show that brutal violence is acceptable to the assailant. But the mugger assumes he will live. When someone wants to die, their disregard for others becomes *slightly* exaggerated, much as Al Qaeda is *slightly* annoying.

A month before and seven months into planning the Columbine Massacre, a pair of psychotic youth began assembling tools of localized mass destruction while videotaping their exit interviews. Eric Harris and Dylan Klebold hunkered in their basements and on camera openly discussed and showcased both the motivation and the means of the most massive school yard assault in American history. They were pumped-up purse snatchers without need for an old lady's pension.

During their videotaped dialogues, Harris and Klebold drank from a bottle of Jack Daniels (naughty and maybe illegal), showed a stack of homemade pipe bombs (against both state and federal law) they called the "Charlie batch" – the Able and Baker batches evidently being stored elsewhere. Harris had a sawed-off shotgun (illegal via federal law since 1934) he named Arlene. He also has a "bandolier of stuff" where he planned to pack homemade napalm (illegal ... period) and they mentioned their large propane tank bombs (very illegal). Mini grenades made of $CO_2$ cartridges and buckshot (way, way, way illegal). The only missing element of their armory were tactical nukes (yes, they are illegal too).

Klebold notes, "I hope we kill 250 of you," and Harris agrees saying, "You all need to die! We need to die, too!"

"We did what we had to do," Klebold said on their final installment.

"If the damn bitch would have just let go I wouldn't have had to beat her up."

On full display is an inhuman pattern so obvious that only Oedipus Rex and the gun control industry could miss it. However, such violent and delusional reality disrupts the gun control industry's basic premise that guns are evil and certain people are not, so they avoid examining either detail. Nearly everyone in America's tangled mass of humanity is peaceful, law abiding and borderline boring. If they want to own a firearm they fill out the forms, pay registration fees, endure waiting periods, buy trigger locks and then never do anything harmful to themselves or other folk. Criminals don't fill out forms, decline to register guns or pay the requisite fee, have no waiting period and wouldn't recognize a trigger lock if it were one of their facial piercings.

Harris and Klebold gamed the system too. On the Columbine Killer Videos, Harris kisses his sawed-off shotgun saying, "Go ahead and change gun laws – how do you think we got ours?"

Self-evident, self-explanatory and an unacceptable narrative for politicians proffering new laws and old promises. This obvious iniquity exists because a different agenda drives the gun control industry. Janet Reno herself said it best. A witness heard her tell a Coral Gables B'nai B'rith meeting, "The most effective means of fighting crime in the United States is to outlaw the possession of *any type of firearm* by the civilian populace."

That certainly worked well in the United Kingdom ...

# Chapter 8: England Is Not Peaceful
(how Rebecca Peters lie)

"Damn the Dutch!" might have been the thought ricocheting through Rebecca Peters' alleged mind.

Peters' hair – Roman emperor styled – must have spiked in porcupine defense when a Dutch government agency statistically kneecapped a primary message of her International Action Network on Small Arms (IANSA), a George Soros subsidized syndicate.[1] In her manic maneuvers to bless the rest of the planet with the Australian-style gun bans that she helped engineer, Peters and her cohorts painted vivid contrasts of how America stood alone as a seething cesspool of incivility in contrast to the rest of the industrialized world. Peters claimed in public debates that the United States contributes "disproportionately to many of the world's problems," insinuating that American bumpkins needed to rise to

---

[1] At press time Ms. Peters had resigned from IANSA, whose web site had fallen into a static state, and her name has not surfaced in news reports since

the level of political sophistication and cosmopolitan safety enjoyed by England, Scotland, Finland, France and her own Australia.

Which, according to those damned Dutch, were significantly more violent places than the U.S.A.

The Dutch Ministry of Justice made the politically incorrect mistake of performing valid research, which as anyone practiced in politics knows is a sure way to have your government grant revoked. Being spitting distance from European capitals plagued with street violence even outside of soccer season, Holland's hoodlum investigators pondered if other industrialized countries were actually more violent, or if that perception was produced by frequent visits to Amsterdam coffee shops (where one cannot find a cup of coffee but can achieve a contact high by reading the menu). They surveyed citizens in seventeen industrialized countries encompassing most of Western Europe, parts of the former Soviet empire and the United States. They counted the number of motorcycle thefts, fraud, vandalisms, burglaries, identity thefts and acts of violence.

Political crimes were omitted since IANSA activities would skew the results.

When the Dutch published their findings, Rebecca Peters could be heard screaming in New York, which is impressive given that IANSA headquarters are in London. Indeed, her London base may have distorted her perspective on violent crime given that the Dutch survey showed disarmed England ranked number two in contact crimes and assaults, ceding first place to Peters' native and largely disarmed Australia.

**The Lie of Distance:** Comparing places to which the average voter has never traveled to create a misleading policy analogy.

Political myth-making relies on imagery. Getting the average citizen to vote in a mayoral election is hard enough. Voting for abstract initiatives or equally abstract candidates is merely impossible. Political operatives thus turn to visualizations in attempts to make legislation tangible. Favorite among people pushing proposals not in the interest of individuals is to make one man's situation appear to be worse than that of everyone else. Cause a chap in Chappaquiddick to believe that his drunk driving conviction will earn him more jail time than a dude in Denver, and you will see a senator relocate to the Mile High city. The inherent problem with this approach is that anyone who can sample the alternative situation will believe his own experience and not what he is told. Let a man live in both Kenilworth and Kansas City and he'll have ample evidence to decide on his own which city is worse.

Reality is highly inconvenient in politics.

Reality has been highly inconvenient to the gun control industry. Since the modern gun control mania began in the 1970s, Peters and other gun prohibitionists have contrasted select locales with strict gun control to other locales with little. Comparisons were commonly drawn between the U.K. and the U.S. As the sun was setting rapidly across the British Empire in the latter 20th century, their Parliament engaged in disarming the populace. Having lived with licensing but without confiscation for centuries (aside from disarming a few Catholics), the Queen's subjects were ill prepared for several rounds of involuntary firearm inventory reductions. This disarmament in turn afforded invalid comparisons between two English-speaking, industrialized nations – with a begrudged admission of common heritage – where one was effectively disarmed while the other was comparatively awash in weaponry. This contrast enabled the gun control industry to compare relatively low homicide rates under The Crown against redneck rampages of lower-caste colonists. Americans who had never traveled to the U.K. or Australia lacked street-level experiences with which to compare the likelihood of violent interactions in London or Lynchburg or Launceston.

Until those damned Dutch disrupted the deception.

According to Australian and American respondents, an Aussie was more than twice as likely to be mugged, sexually assaulted or beaten to a bloody pulp than a Yank. English and Welsh residents were marginally better off, having *almost* double the number of violent encounters. Less forcible offences – like attempted burglary – had similar international gaps to further perturb Peters. Data showed that Australian criminals – including Liberal Party Prime Ministers – were violently hyperactive compared to their lazier American peers.

Or perhaps American thugs were simply forced to contemplate which of their potential victims might be armed.

Peters was not the only politico perplexed that their primary prevarication was put to rest. Residents of Australia, England, Wales, Scotland, Canada, Finland, Poland, Northern Ireland, Denmark, France, Sweden, Switzerland and, yes, the Netherlands were riled upon discovering that they were subject to violence rates higher than that of the evil United States. The Dutch Ministry of Justice left only Japan, Portugal, Spain and Belgium with non-violent bragging rights, and Belgians weren't snickering given their virtual tie with America. Aside from the Swiss – a well armed nation intent on keeping IRS investigators out of their country – Europe's hodgepodge of gun control initiatives proved unfavorable to commoners. The Dutch criminalization survey indicated no correlation between civilian ownership rates of firearms and violent crime. Scatterguns produce more tightly grouped patterns than scatter diagrams of violent crime versus gun control laws throughout the world.

Which is why Rebecca Peters never looks at the entire world. Cherry picking populations is her ploy to traduce more peaceful countries.

**The Lie of Selected Cells:** Selecting a small number (often two) points of

**reference to create a false comparison, ignoring the remaining combinations.**

Throughout the world different countries have either a little gun control or a lot of gun control, and they have either low violent crime rates or high violent crime rates. You can find at least one country to fit in any given cell of this four-part matrix. Strict gun control and low crime: Japan. Loose gun control and low crime: Switzerland. Strict gun control and high crime: Russia, Mexico, Columbia, Jamaica, England, Wales, Scotland, Australia ...

Intentional failure to examine or report all possible combinations of cause and effect is central to lobbing larger lies. Two functions of falsehood are involved. First of course is Maier's Law of Research, which states, "If the facts do not conform to the theory, the facts must be disposed of." Inconvenient truths work against legislative theory. Second, and perhaps more importantly, is that simple, stark contrasts are more communicative. Black vs. white. Liberal vs. conservative. Sane vs. Congress. Politicos distill selected data into small, repeatable talking points specifically so humans and reporters will parrot them. Slick, non-salient talking points move faster than a K-Street lobbyist at a GOP fund raiser.

Few move faster than simple, false dualities.

These mendacious methods are practiced on micro as well as macro scales. Contrast Compton with Crown Heights and one might well call for banning Compton itself, not to mention guns in general. But compare Manhattan with Midlothian and the good people of Richmond, Virginia's lower west side will keep their guns and build barriers to contain Manhattan and the Bronx as well. Yet the gun control industry uses selected single-variable evaluations to bypass the average voter's analytical attention span. People have barely enough time to scan the headlines before herding children to soccer matches or heading themselves to the firing range (no, not downtown Compton).

**The Lie of Exotic Divergence:** Contrasting two items without exploring everything that might cause their differences.

Folks from Compton, the Bronx and Midlothian are similar in exactly the same way as ostrich, antelope and horse fish. In Compton you are likely black, in the Bronx you have high odds of being Italian, and in restive Midlothian they refuse to answer intrusive inquiries from the meddling Census Bureau. Compton residents make 20% less than the national average. So do people on East 159th Street, but they eat better. Nobody in Midlothian has voluntarily reported income since the Nixon administration. Regional ratios of single parent households, employment rates and ACLU membership are also bearing factors on what causes locals to commit acts of violence. Volumes of variables must be evaluated before rational conclusions are codified.

Which is why they aren't.

Politics is the exercise of power. Rational people prefer to retain as much power as possible, ceding it only when the alternative stinks. Anarchy sounds good on paper until you realize you have to be your own cop, fireman and sanitation engineer. Tossing tax dollars and a tiny amount of choice to a central authority for pooled services occasionally makes sense. However, people become ornery as the power they are asked to release grows. In order to effect change that is not in the interest of the individual, the individual must first believe that the deal offered is a better solution than self-reliance. Ask folk in Compton if they have seen a homicide and want gun control, and a lot of hands will go up. Ask people in Midlothian about homicides and they'll scratch their skulls trying to recall the last one, though they can recite off the top of their heads the mean velocity of a 185 grain .45 caliber round and the last burglar to catch one.

Comparing all possible variables is non-trivial. Even university-entrapped economists argue about which variables matter, the source and reliability of the raw data, arcane statistical tests and calculations, and why they can't find a date for Saturday night. Complex multi-regional population comparisons apply within a single nation, but more importantly when contrasting Kiwis with Canucks. Assuming that variables like income and indoor plumbing are equal across nations, or that such demographic variations have no effect on crime is slightly less sound than a Charlie Rangel alibi.

Which brings us back to the U.K. and the nature of violence. Different cultures enjoy different forms of mayhem. Mexican drug lords have adopted the Jihadist beheading habit. Rwandans don't bother severing heads though the implements used in their genocide campaigns are similar to the Mexican mafia and Taliban traditionalist. Dutch criminological number crunchers show that Brits are very fond of violent assault though less fond of homicide itself. In modern times folks in England, Wales and Scotland are twice as likely to be physically accosted as an American, though Americans are six times more likely to be murdered.

Brits used to have it better.

Subjects of the Empire may be more prone to random acts of violence but have always been less likely to take violence to fatal conclusions, where as Americans drive bargains harder and kill more casually. Yet, when examining homicide data for the past century, two interesting things come to light: First, Brits have always had a lower homicide rate, even when they had wide-open access to firearms. Second, British homicide rates continue to rise after effectively banning firearms while America's homicide rates dropped during the same period.

## The Lie of Limited Perspective:
Avoidance of exposing the big picture
or long-range trends.

Rebecca Peters doesn't talk about homicide trends in the U.K. or Australia, as they have done the opposite of the gun control industry's predictions. Between 1960 and 2000 (selected to include modern drug prohibition and gun control enactments) the U.K. and the USofA saw a rise in homicides in the first three of those decades. The U.K. enacted ever more stringent gun control laws prohibiting semi-automatic and pump-action center fire rifles, short shotguns with magazines, and pump- or self-loading rifles (1988) and effectively eliminating handguns (1997). Reacting to a similar growing rate of street crime, 41 American states began allowing non-criminal citizens to carry handguns in public and doubling the supply of handguns in circulation. Homicide rates in the U.K. shot up about 30% and homicides in the U.S. fell about 50% between 1980 and 2000.

Firearm crime rates are also rising in the U.K., which is odd for a disarmed society.

Legislation is allegedly enacted to cause an effect. Rebecca Peters' reaction to tragic violence with a gun was to ban guns with the intent of reducing the level of violence. If violence rises instead of abating, the rational deduction is that her gun bans did not have the intended effect. Naturally the solution offered by Rebecca Peters, Sarah Brady and the fellow who wants to burgle your home tonight is to ban even more of those inanimate objects. If banning handguns increased crime, then ban shotguns. If banning shotguns escalated violence, then ban air guns. If eliminating private ownership of air guns increases crime, then ban blow guns, cap guns, water pistols, lawn darts, Legos that can be joined to look like a gun, toy soldiers and Hello Kitty dolls (well, that last one might be worth banning).

The final solution is banning people, which some brown shirts once tried.

This process of perpetually expanding demonstrable stupidity is known as the "Fatal Attraction to Failed Ideas," according to political philosopher and firearms aficionado Ralph Seifert. Seifert's theorem holds that the political cost of admitting that a favorite legislative theory has failed is so large that activists will proffer more of the same lest their original victory be stripped bare and political capital lost. People more cynical than Seifert – an extremely small club – believe that the gun control industry has an end game and thus the rationality of their legislation or the results thereof are immaterial. The objective of eliminating private firearm ownership is unhindered by comparative data showing that firearm bans increase violence. Violence prevention was never the concern of the prohibitionist, merely the faulty justification for encouraging people to surrender a specific freedom. In order to effect change that is not in the interest of the individual, the individual must first believe that the deal offered is a better solution.

Rational people must be duped to forsake the tools of survival.

Which brings us back to the perpetually tragic tale of Rebecca Peters and her minions in IANSA. Peters is intimate with the cause and effect of gun bans. She was the chair of Australia's National Coalition for Gun Control when a madman became devilish in Tasmania, shooting up the historic Port Author prison. Peters was the Manipulator and Chief of a campaign to denude Australians of their guns. After engineering a forced sale of firearms to the government, and sticking Australian tax payers with a tab of $500M Australian bucks, Peters bugged-out for England leaving Aussies to suffer increased assault, armed robbery rates and other forms of involuntary violent interactions.

Peters now wants the rest of the world to benefit, as have her former friends in Australia.

In a gleaming multi-story building in London's upper east side, IANSA coordinates the actions of over 800 organizations dotting the globe. The main mission is expansion and propagation of a United Nations initiative to create federated control over firearms. The UN Small Arms Conference seeks to define the role of every government in a coordinated effort to restrict who can have guns (whoever is in power) and who cannot (the subservient masses). IANSA's jejune mission statement portrays a positive spin on how government will make things as cheery in Portland as they are in Port Arthur.

"...IANSA seeks to make people safer from gun violence by securing *stronger regulation* on guns in society ... IANSA will continue to play a leadership role in the UN Small Arms Conference process and will remain actively engaged in its *Control Arms campaign* during the development process of a UN Arms Trade Treaty ... IANSA will raise and maintain the profile of the small arms crisis ... IANSA will engage and *coordinate media outreach* efforts to promote ... to wider audiences." (emphasis quite obviously not theirs)

**The Lie of Vague Intentions:** Uttering ill-defined but popular objectives while striving for specific and unpopular goals.

Comedians and politicians have one unifying trait aside from high rates of alcoholism. They know their audiences and adapt to each. Rebecca's marketing staff knows that non-specific platitudes are appropriate for the IANSA web site. Rebecca knows that leaking details is important when talking to her base. While her staff whispers sweet nothings about the horrors of genocide into the ears of the media, Rebecca can occasionally be caught disclosing details of her end game to more friendly audiences. While cuddling a correspondent with the Ploughshares Monitor, the ever-unctuous Peters lamented her limited success in subverting the already subversive machinery of the United Nations. While dubiously declaring that "...disputes where previously law-abiding but armed citizens lose their tempers" were a significant source of firearm carnage, she expressed disappointment that she had failed in creating "a global legal instrument on marking, recordkeeping, and tracing" and that the UN "instrument ... is not legally binding but only voluntary, and does not cover ammunition." Most bitterly she bemoaned that the UN's Programme of Action "... doesn't attempt to regulate the civilian use of small arms ... and it neglects the problem of arms transfers to non-state actors," e.g., civilians.

In other words, she prefers that only governments have guns, as in Rwanda, Uganda, Bosnia, Darfur and Berlin ghettos.

The rhetorical ravine between the professed desire for "stronger regulation" and the end game of keeping guns solely in the hands the state is one Robbie Knievel wouldn't dare jump. Segregating audiences and messages is an elegant form of political fibbery that is rapidly withering due to inexpensive, highly portable recording devices and the mass distribution network that is the Internet. When millions of people with policy acumen and a lot of spare time can obtain, transcribe, share and analyze every statement made by practitioners of the dark art of political flummery, linguistic deceptions are rapidly disrobed. Peer-to-peer analysis leaks into the public, influencing voters not in the hyper-political caste. Marketing gurus know that people trust neighbors and family more than the media, a byproduct of decades of misleading advertising and New York Times reporting. The media must cater to the thirty-second attention span, and as a result tend to regurgitate the thirty-second sound bites offered by Rebecca Peters and associated succubi. An unintended consequence of lackluster journalism and unending Internet analysis is that the established media's reputation is soaring at the same lofty altitudes as whale excrement.

Which brings us back to the Dutch and their inconvenient assessment of multinational violence. When released, their study caused sedated academics and a few uninebriated reporters to take notice. Dutch criminological headlines denied the prevailing spin, which in and of itself made for an interesting news item. Since most of modern Europe is more violent than the well armed United States, other elements than firearms were surely involved in the crime calculus. Normative human behavior was one such element. Compton residents fear the Crips because street gangs have guns and an utter disregard for human life. Midlothian residents have guns, respect for life and fear nothing because they only shoot burglars. Overnight Holland's Ministry of Justice recalibrated international understanding of the source of violence regardless of the tools of carnage. In unguarded moments, even Rebecca Peters' pals get it.

Rebecca herself is still a lost cause.

Mark Grigorian is one of Peters' protégées, speaking on behalf of the Institute for War and Peace, which despite its name is not a Tolstoy reading club. While addressing a United Nations Biennial Meeting of States, Grigorian asserted that the Crips have intellectual kinship with governments around the world. "In Jamaica independent reports cite over 600 suspected unlawful killings of civilians by police ... The period before Cambodia's February 2002 local elections was marred by political killings and intimidation by armed men. In one province, two opposition party members were shot at point-blank range by men wearing military uniforms in November 2001. This was followed by a campaign of armed intimidation by assailants armed with AK-47 assault rifles. The prime suspects are law enforcement and military officers closely associated with local authorities."

Yet Rebecca bemoans that the UN "doesn't attempt to regulate the civilian use of small arms ... and it neglects the problem of arms transfers to non-state actors."

Criminals and politicians are two large, active and incestuous teams. Their pathological similarities extend to their relationship with the general population. Naked force is a primary tool for gaining and keeping control of other people, and historically both groups have been most effective when they are the only ones who can use it. A cop in Kingstown, a

Blood in Boston, a Janjaweed in Janub all thrive because they have all the firepower and no remorse. A mechanic in Midlothian has firepower but also a set of values that dictate his more peaceable ways. Statisticians and recovering reporters recognize that the control variable is not guns but culture.

> **The Lie of Humanitarianism:** Appealing to people's hopes that aberrant human behavior can be post-processed, and later enforced, by government.

Sem Peng Seam beat Mark Grigorian to the podium at the same UN biannual meeting. Seam comes from Cambodia, a nation that saw a couple of million people vanish thanks to Pol Pot's enthusiastic community-organizing efforts (e.g., if you did not want to join an agrarian community, you died). Seam rattled off a laundry list of motives the average Mongkol or Midlothian resident might have to own a firearm. Among his index of incentives for obtaining self-defense tools were the issues of inadequate public safety, police brutality and human rights abuses. Nothing like watching 26% of your country's population disappear to limit your liking of government's helping hand.

Yet Rebecca is unstoppable. After Seam, Grigorian and six other activists spoke at the UN conference, Rebecca took the stage to summarize IANSA's use of the UN, asserting that they should "adopt strict arms export criteria that are based on the observance of human rights and compliance with international humanitarian law."

Which includes the UN's Universal Declaration of Human Rights, which isn't universal and is oddly lacking in some basic human rights. Nowhere in the eight pages and thirty articles does the UN cite a right to self-defense much less a right to the tools thereof. The UN assures everyone that they have a "right to life, liberty and security of person" but not the means to guarantee it. Nor does the declaration lead to enforcement of the sundry rights, leaving it to the good faith and altruistic nature of governments, like UN Human Rights Council member states Djibouti (arbitrary arrest, prisoner abuse, female genital mutilation), Jordan (torture, honor killings, speech suppression), Malaysia (vote suppression, religious suppression, indefinite detention), Mexico (uncontrolled drug-related violence, mass governmental corruption, rampant kidnapping), Nigeria (politically motivated killings, lethal force against suspects, beatings and torture of suspects, extortion of civilians, human trafficking), Russia (reporter assassinations, systematic torture, dissident internment in psychiatric institutions), Saudi Arabia (where to begin), Cuba (where does it end) and China (there is no end).

Intellectually corrupt chimeras like Rebecca can keep two interrelated atrocities separated in their seemingly psychotic minds. She supports governments keeping arms, but not people. Rebecca chooses to leave unreported centuries of evidence that such lopsided enforcement results not in civil society but in genocide. She is quite clear that people in Midlothian and victims in Darfur should not have the means to protect themselves. In a debate at Kings College she said (and edited out of the transcripts on the IANSA web site), "Yes, I believe that semiautomatic rifles and shotguns have no legitimate role in civilian hands. And not only that, handguns have no legitimate role in civilian hands." She needs to chat with the few surviving Cambodians besides Sem Peng Seam.

Or a few Mexicans.

Mexico is a country of interesting beauty and institutionalized crime. When Tom Lehrer sang of Mexico's bull fights and dysentery, he also sang of his wallet being lifted. Common advice to newbie travelers is to take plenty of cash for bribing the police who otherwise inconvenience visitors with short jail stays. A national election cannot be held in Mexico without top government officials being blamed for, proven to be and elected for being slightly less corrupt than his opponent. A good day in Guadalajara is one where you stay out of jail, have bus fare home, are not kidnapped for ransom or be-headed by one of the kindlier drug cartel members.

Mexico is so mired in drug trafficking violence that Compton Crips don't dare visit Veracruz. With an estimated $40 billion in annual revenues, growing American demand and a complete disregard for law and life, Mexican drug lords practice violence with the same daily discipline as Rebecca Peters practices perjury.

Which is slightly less often than Dianne Feinstein.

"It is unacceptable to have 90% of the guns that are picked up in Mexico and used to shoot judges, police officers, mayors, kidnap innocent people and do terrible things come from the United States," was Feinstein's sinister-sounding homily. She sat surrounded by fellow Senatorial sanitarium inmates aping the sound bite while a representative from the Bureau of Alcohol, Tobacco, Firearms and Explosives (BATFE) tried to slide more realistic information into the record and before the cameras. Dianne was having none of that, artfully deflecting the BATFE rebuttals and repeating the 90% sound bite until even veteran Capitol Hill reporters began snoring.

> **The Lie of Slices:** Using a small slice of data to simultaneously obscure the reality presented by all the available data, and creating a false sense of blame.

Mexican drug cartels are not your friendly neighborhood dope dealers. They are large, wealthy, multinational operations with private armies. The Mexican cartels have annual incomes that exceed the GDP of neighboring Guatemala and 129 other countries around the world. All of their employees are, by definition, working criminals as are their global trade associates. Combine criminality, wealth and ruthlessness and you have George Soros, or at very least the Sinaloa Cartel. Mexico's drug lords can shop the world for product and supplies, and it appears that they do. Browse news reports about Mexican drug violence, and some interesting armament is routinely mentioned. There are hand grenades in Guerrero, RPGs in Rosarito, armor-piercing munitions in Manzanillo and anti-tank rockets in Aguascalientes. Each item has two commonalities – they are military weapons of war and none are available in American gun stores. Why buy hunting rifles in Laredo when you can purchase rocket-propelled grenades directly from China?

Or, have corrupt members of the Mexican government forward shipments of U.S. Army M-16s sent to fight the War on Drugs.

"It is unacceptable to have 90% of the guns that are picked up in Mexico and used to shoot judges, police officers, mayors, kidnap innocent people and do terrible things come from the United States," Feinstein repeated from hilltop to web site to the wilds of San Francisco.

To understand Dianne's deceit, we have to understand the Lie of Slices. The BATFE helps government agencies by tracing the serial numbers of guns found at crime scenes (which may or may not have been used in a crime, but were picked up during a bust). The BATFE then searches a database to determine which federally licensed gun dealer bought each weapon from the manufacturer. No further information is available in traces and BATFE staff members are too busy enduring Senate interrogations to do law enforcement work.

Only firearms that government agencies ask to be traced are traced. Firearms that are not traced are not included in BATFE reporting. The datum Dianne diligently dissected from the larger pool of information was not in error, but her phrasing of it intentionally was. Perhaps 90% of firearms the Mexican government asked the American government to trace were originally retailed in the United States. Yet Feinstein insisted that "90% of the guns that are *picked up in Mexico*" were. The empty gulf between the number of crime guns recovered and the number traced through the BATFE database is as vast as the empty gulf between Dianne's left and right ear lobes.

The Mexican attorney general's office reported seizing 29,000 weapons throughout 2007 and 2008. Of these 11,000 (38%) resulted in a trace request to the BATFE. Of the firearms that the American agency investigated, about 6,000 (21%) could be successfully traced and 5,114 (18%) were confirmed as having been sold in America. Close to 90% of *traced* guns came from America, but less than 18% of *reported seized* guns did. Missing from the data is the true scope of the weapons found or admitted to by the Mexican government. In the land of institutionalized corruption, the odds are relatively high that guns trafficked through the government and to the cartels are not reported nor would it be worth their time to ask the BATFE to trace the origins of a U.S. Army M-16 that is unavailable to U.S. citizens.

Not to mention the Russian- and Chinese-made AK-47s, RPGs and anti-tank missiles. But that would not meet their symbiotic objectives. Thus the Lie of Slices is as intrinsic to Dianne Feinstein and Rebecca Peters' work as 50 peso bribes are to Cancun cops.

# Chapter 9: Social Costs and Guns
(how Barack Obamas lie)

"Tax bullets?" replied the cop as he donned hearing protec-
tors, chambered a round in his Glock and prepared to toss a
few rounds down an alley at the San Leandro Rifle Range.
"The government should subsidize them. Give citizens a
Homeland Defense bullet rebate."

Clearly this cop had not read any of the academic research
into the social cost of guns. Poor fellow had to rely only upon
what he saw daily on the rough streets of Oakland, California.

Ivy-covered professors are curious creatures who through
deep and diligent study manage to get a great many things
wrong. They avoid small error while sweeping on to grander
fallacies. It is a side effect of a silly and somewhat dysfunc-
tional system. Academics must produce something tangible
lest research grant monies vanish faster than coed sobriety
and virginity, which might make for an interesting research
project itself. Even proper professors have been known to
distort rational research methodologies when their initial
investigations yield nothing interesting, which by definition

means something controversial. When money from political prostitution rings masquerading as charitable foundations enters the academic mix, researchers with supple scruples will invent a dozen new and exotic statistical fallacies before lunch.

Enter "social cost" justifications for legislation.

From political stage left comes the quaint and curious notion that chartered republics (i.e., your federal and state governments) are in the business of balancing liberty and social issues using calculated social costs and benefits. No less of a mind than that of Supreme Court Jester Stephen Breyer – and there are few minds lesser than his – squandered 44 pages of dissenting perfidy arguing that the confirmed constitutional right of Americans to own firearms had to be balanced against perceived social costs. Ignore judicial dementia and that fossilized magistrates have never been authorized to plop civil rights and economics on Lady Justice's scales. Larger questions loom.

Such as, "Does Lady Justice wear that blindfold to avoid looking directly at Steven Breyer?"

"Social costs" is a concept as firm and well rooted as Sahara sand. Some interpret social costs to be direct financial costs to individuals. Other folk think it is out-of-pocket government expenses including welfare, indigent medical care and congressional bourbon therapy. Berkeley residents still riddled with psilocybin from their last Grateful Dead road trip perceive more spiritual expenses before subsequent hallucinogenic experiences overtake them. The definition of social costs is as precise as that for "assault weapons," both definitions being as narrow as nuclear weapon target diameters. Quantifying social costs is nearly impossible.

Which has not deterred a few abased academics.

**The Lie of Cost:** Using arbitrary and inconsistent definitions of cost to create a false impression of a serious problem.

"Cost" is one of those lissom English words that evoke different meanings for different people, and there is no nation with people more different than the United States (only America could produce both Elvis and Lady Gaga). "Cost" to the accountant at Jim's Feed and Supply of Klaflin, Kansas is vastly different than the "cost" a mother pays when burying her former gangsta son. Yet certain academics – most without the necessary chops – have attempted to quantify the actual financial cost of the misuse of guns.

An early example of "social cost" academic alchemy appeared in the *Annals of Internal Medicine*, an odd place to peddle a paper dealing with statistical economics. Linda Gunderson, bored with writing about mere medical matters, slid nearly undetected into economics, criminology and infamy. Published along with research on paroxysmal nocturnal hemoglobinuria cells and fire ant attacks on residents in health care facilities, the *Annals of Internal Medicine* pushed her piece claiming that on the high end America spent about $100 billion bucks mopping up the mess left by gunfire. Based on 1996 data, the alleged cost of owning guns in the U.S. was over 1% of that year's national GDP, a figure large enough to make even Barack Obama blink.

Gruderson's groundwork met the primary objective of the gun control industry: It lobbed a staggering claim about the alleged evil of guns with a succinct sound bite that reporters could toss blindly into their broadcast echo chamber. The mind-numbingly large dollar amount (mind numbing in pre-Fannie Mae bailout perspective) was rapidly echoed by such disreputable bodies as the Brady Campaign and the Pennsylvania Department of Public Welfare. Such a large portion of U.S. wealth going to the ravages of gun violence caught everyone's attention and caused Justice Breyer to wet his robes.

It also caught the attention of working criminologists and economists who wet themselves laughing.

As with "assault weapons" the devil was in the definitions. Most folk perceive "cost" as the direct exchange of money for something, be it a can of Coke or a gram of coke. "Cost" can also be the direct price of fixing something such as the gaping wound that a rival gang member made in your torso with his knife. These costs are fixed and limited to the duration of the exchange. If the price you paid for a single can of Coke was multiplied over months and years, you would switch to Pepsi.

> **The Lie of Duration:** Not exposing the duration of the topic in order to inflate or deflate the apparent cost, risk or benefit.

Economists, looking for something better to do than brood over their empty social calendars, dashed off critiques of the $100 billion estimates noting – with sneering derision the likes of which only economists are capable on a Saturday night – that the figure included lost incomes of criminals killed by law-abiding citizens or by other criminals. Evidently crime does pay since gang bangers lose lifetime incomes totaling billions of bucks, a fact which has stoked fits of financial jealously in less talented larcenists in Congress. Gunderson herself noted that 85% of the estimated financial effect of guns "was for premature death (lost productivity)."

Busy little drug dealers.

Half of the remaining "social costs of guns" were racked up in medical treatments, which without citation Gunderson claims are born primarily by the taxpayer. Granted, gang members typically carry inadequate health insurance. When an ambulance wheels a Norteños or Vice Lords member into ER, few hospitals bother asking for payment in advance. Since government is disbarred from discriminating on the basis of race, creed or gang colors, hospitals repair the damage and bill you. In Obama's Chicago – where handguns were until recently banned – gangland shootings are frequent to the point that emergency room staffs want to tattoo bar codes on gang member foreheads to speed in-processing.

This is the foundation of Obama's universal health care program, though you have the option of putting your tattoo inside your forearm.

Lost lifetime earnings potential of dead delinquents stretches the definition of "social costs" to extremes reminiscent of Barney Frank's girdle. Unlike fractious Frank's girth, everything else has a limit. Death terminates social interaction and simultaneously terminates both the income and expenses of the corpse. Including truncated incomes of deceased drug dealers in "social cost" equations assumes that the income will not be earned by someone else. This applies not only to departed desperados but to people so annoyed with life that they voluntarily opt out. Most "social cost" studies include the forfeited future incomes of the successfully suicidal, which make up nearly 60% of people who intercept bullets.

**The Lie of Blindness:** Willingly repeating factoids that have been disproven in order to perpetuate the myth.

Yes, certain medical academics attempted to quantify the financial cost of the misuse of guns, which other academics – who specialize in and stick to their own fields of study – rapidly debunked. Gunderson was not alone in being intellectually barbequed by economists. Most "social costs" papers suffered from congenital defects that were passed on from one ill-begotten study to the next. Unknotting the pipeline of academic effluvium has kept a lot of people profitably busy on the other side of campus.

They toiled to little avail. While America's foremost former civil rights group – the NAACP – was campaigning against the civil right to own firearms, they cited Gunderson's paper in their amicus brief to the Supreme Court on the pivotal Heller case, and thus gave Justice Breyer the necessary ore for demonstrating senility and dissent. Despite a near decade of lambasting, these "social cost" studies were piled before the highest of courts and infected the thinking of sitting judges. Justice Breyer's scales became as unbalanced as he.

### The Lie of Balance: Avoiding exposure of the opposite assumption in order to avoid providing balanced perspective.

If guns create a huge social cost, then two perspective-granting elements must be examined. First and horrifically amusing are other forms of carnage, but ones that lack unconstitutional end games. Politicians in New Orleans – the same cabal that failed to reinforce their own levies, allowed mass looting and forcibly disarmed their residents in the apocalyptic aftermath of hurricane Katrina – tried suing gun manufacturers for crimes those companies did not commit. Civic shysters made much of the number of children who died accidentally from gunfire. In New Orleans lower wards this was commonly from assassinations, either by street gangs or the New Orleans Police Department, though such cross-organizational distinctions are fuzzy. In nearly the same year that Gunderson peddled her paper, the CDC said that less than 0.001% of kids died from any form of gunfire much less the subset of accidental shootings. More than three times as many drowned, but the NAACP didn't complain about that until after the levies broke. Sixty-one times as many kids were beaten to death, but Gunderson was oddly indifferent to their lost future incomes. Suffocation caused the death of 491 times as many pre-pubescents, but Justice Breyer failed to balance those tragic episodes with the right to keep and bear plastic bags.

The other uninspected angle is the social *benefit* that gun ownership provides. Everything – aside from Henry Waxman – has a potential social benefit. If Justice Breyer were serious about his unauthorized balancing act, he would calculate the net social cost *and* benefit to an armed populace. A person of intellect (which disqualifies Justice Breyer and other bench bimbi) would ponder the role of guns outside criminal enterprises.

Which is precisely why they don't.

**The Lie of Unexamined Alternatives:** Examining only half of an obviously two-sided discussion to keep people from obtaining a full perspective.

Gary Kleck is an interesting anomaly in criminology. Laboring in that tropical Hell called Florida, Kleck resembles the bastard child of Jimmy Buffet and Arlo Guthrie. He stands out from the academic crowds not only in his casual appearance, but also in his casual way of discussing homicide, rape, assault and other recreations. Kleck is persona non grata to the gun control industry for the blatant error of doing what Gunderson and Breyer would not. Kleck and his cohorts conducted their own survey – and gathered together other surveys carried out by criminologists and the media – seeking data on when, how and how often people used guns to prevent the homicides, rapes and assaults he so casually discusses. He sought to understand what value the American public derives from not dying or being defiled, or from putting robbers on the run. Kleck had a hunch there might possibly be some social benefit to private ownership of firearms and that they might upon occasion be justifiably used.

Two and a half million times a year is the cross-study consensus – a number as frighteningly large to the gun control industry as $100 billion was to juiced justices.

In 1996, the same year of study as Gunderson's social costs canard, there were 458,457 police-documented violent crimes with firearms in the United States (for detail-oriented readers that figure includes 13,319 murders, 218,579 robberies and

226,559 aggravated assaults, though nobody recorded any blissful assaults). These are successful violent altercations that police recorded, though there are an unknown number of unreported incidents. Thus, on the bottom end of the respective ranges – gun crimes and crime preventions using guns – roughly five times as many acts of violence were prevented because the victim was armed and the criminal was not quite as dumb as he looked.

A 5X social benefit of private gun ownership is the estimated imbalance. The cop was right, tax-subsidized bullet rebates are justified.

However, this is an apples to kumquats comparison. Gunderson guessed at dollar costs, so we must extrapolate the dollar savings from active self-defense. Her analysis self-admittedly focused on large urban centers, which oddly is where street gangs keep their headquarters. By bifurcating Gunderson's analysis and applying her statistical indiscretions to surviving suburbanites as well as dead inner-city gangsters, we come closer to achieving the balance Justice Breyer studiously avoided. While grinding through his survey tallies, Kleck discovered that about 400,000 of your neighbors claimed that a gun dissuaded their attacker and "almost certainly" saved a life. Any given year there are fewer than 10,000 firearm homicides. The Bureau of Justice Statistics claims around 94% of these are gang related and mainly occur in the large cities to which Linda Gunderson restricted her study. This means more than forty times the number of honest citizens save themselves from thuggary than the number of Crips gunned down by Bloods, Bloods capped by Crips, or even actresses shot by Phil Spector.

Looking at just body-count-adjusted cost/savings, private gun ownership provides forty times more social benefit than the social cost of gangland misuse of firearms. The social savings are actually more since the annual earning potential and longevity of suburbanites is larger and longer than anyone running with the Dog Town Rifa. The lifetime earnings of

400,000 middle class non-victims are significantly higher than the lost wages of gangsta ghosts.

Oddly, average people rarely shoot their assailants. Gun owners show amazing restraint, shooting their assaulters less than 1% of the time when a gun is used at all. Perhaps this is the real social cost problem – not enough thugs are experiencing premature loss of productivity. Restrained as they may be, civilians manage to remove far more felons from society than do cops because unlike the police, the victim is always present at the scene of the crime. Kleck, the perpetually inconvenient criminologist that he is, estimates that in a bad year (1990 was his benchmark) upwards of 3,200 felons discover corporal karma. Another 18,500 are legally wounded and if not incarcerated, are certainly rethinking their career options (there is always a vacant seat for them on the Oakland, California City Council). Either way, the net social benefit derived from shunting the career of a criminal is not accounted for in most "social cost" studies.

Not that Barack Obama complains about the oversight. He paid hard cash for it.

In Chicago, in a Madison Street lair littered with lawyers, sits the fashionable offices of the Joyce Foundation. Created by an heir to the David "Lumber Baron" Joyce fortune, this foundation does what all foundations do – bestow gobs of cash upon whatever social issues the founder or latter-day director favor. Originally chartered to endow "religious, charitable, scientific, literary and educational purposes," the Joyce Foundation has given to many causes. They have dabbled in education, the environment, arts and campaign finance.

They also fund the gun control industry.

It is difficult to imagine the American gun control industry surviving a week without the largess of the Joyce Foundation. Seemingly every major gun prohibitionist group is a Joyce habitué, having or continuing to receive funds from this Chicago perjury pump primer. There is the annual stipend to the Violence Policy Center, which invented the previously unknown "assault weapon" category and has the stated goal of confusing the public with the very term it coined. Recurring grants go to San Francisco's Legal Community Against Violence, charged with inventing new gun control laws. Joyce also endows the Entertainment Industries Council and prods them to give Hollywood anti-gun talking points to include in the movies and television programming you watch. Some stimulus goes to the National Opinion Research Center to assure that a selection of gun-related questions is included in allegedly unbiased polling. Hard cash is handed to Handgun-Free America to coordinate and support anti-gun education efforts on college campuses. They also let New York Mayor Michael Bloomberg keep his billions by not having to give grubstake to his own Mayors Against Illegal Guns Coalition organization and their campaign to recruit big city mayors in demanding ever more gun control.

Invent a problem, devise laws, aggregate agitprop, popularize through the media, rig a survey, recruit your kids and pull the strings of political puppets. Yes, the game *is* fixed and has been for a very long time.

**The Lie of Synchronicity:** Creating the appearance of mass, spontaneous mutual consensus to cause the public to believe there is an urgent issue to be resolved.

Cluttering the Joyce Foundation's online listing of "gun violence" grants are gifts-with-strings to the Boston University School of Public Health, Harvard University School of Public Health, Johns Hopkins University School of Hygiene and Public Health (renamed the Bloomberg School of Public Health in honor of Mayor Michael Bloomberg who also contributed heavily), New York Academy of Medicine and the National Foundation for the Centers for Disease Control & Prevention. Joyce money routinely appears at the nexus of gun control politics and medical academics misfiring as criminologists. Throughout the era of "guns as an epidemic" research, the Joyce Foundation was financially associated with grants given to medical institutions or individuals who produced work of little or no criminological merit much less statistical validity, methodological soundness, sanity or scruples. To believe Joyce's "guns as an epidemic" carom canard, to proclaim that hunks of pig iron are pathogens, requires a malfunctioning mind.

Speaking of Barack ...

Eight years is a long time. It is a long time to sit in a prison cell or the Oval Office. It is a very long time to wait for a heart transplant. For many folks it is too long to wait for the Second Coming. Eight years, however, was the amount of time Barack Obama spent on the board of the Joyce Foundation. In one of the few American cities to ban guns outright – except in the case of mobsters, drug-running gangs and select Chicago politicians, a triple redundancy – Obama helped define the Joyce Foundation's donation agenda. According to other board members and the foundation's president, Obama was engaged, studied grant briefing books and was allegedly well prepared during board meetings. In the years where Joyce Foundation gun violence programs were primarily focused on the public health hoax, board approval was typically unanimous.

Obama was closer to the Joyce Foundation agenda than Bill was to Monica.

During his tenure in that camarilla, Obama helped pushed more than two million bucks into the Violence Policy Center. Being studied, prepared and engaged as he reportedly was, Obama did not fail to miss details or the over-arching purpose of those grants. In the same year that fewer than a Million Moms were Marching and the State of Maryland instigated their failed ballistic fingerprinting program, the Violence Policy Center begat a beast titled "Unsafe in Any Hands: Why America Needs to Ban Handguns" and claimed therein as "pure myth" that such a ban was unconstitutional. The foundation's investing theme was amplified that same year when the directors of the Joyce Foundation lobbed an additional $20,000 to support the publication of a Violence Policy Center byproduct – a book titled "Every Handgun is Aimed at You: The Case for Banning Handguns."

"I have always believed that the Second Amendment protects the right of individuals to bear arms," was Obama's 2008 campaign communiqué. Good thing he didn't put the Joyce Foundation's money where his mouth is.

# Chapter 10: States'Rights, The Law That Never Was
(how Pete Starks lie)

Fortney "Pete" Stark is more interesting than other politicians or trolls.

Despite holding a Congressional seat for more years than his constituents care to confess, Stark has developed a progressive lack of humility or intelligence. Pete has been openly hostile to fellow Congress critters and once ran interference in Senate chambers to help rig a vote. He belittled his colleagues for voting to "get [soldier's] heads blown off for the President's amusement." He called a sitting African American presidential cabinet member "a disgrace to his race." Stark called a fellow Congressman "Field Marshal Solarz in the pro-Israel forces" while blaming his "Jewish colleagues" for the Persian Gulf War. Stark called one Congresswoman a "whore for the insurance industry" and in committee tried to instigate a fist fight with a fellow California representative, calling him a "little wimp" and "you little fruitcake."

Normally, unattractive and emotionally bereft people compensate by developing *likable* personalities.

Not Pete. Nor are Stark's incivilities limited to beltway barnacles. He has taken aim at his own constituents – his employers if you will. He replied to one voter's correspondence with scorn in a voicemail message saying, "I doubt if you could spell half the words in [your] letter" and "you tell me more about why you think you're such a great goddamn hero." The digital revolution somehow had escaped Stark's notice for he never contemplated the possibility that the voicemail he left on a Silicon Valley constituent's phone would be instantly relayed to every talk radio program in America.

A different constituent caused Petey to expose his ignorance of the Constitution as well as his inability to read. Stark has favored gun control since his younger brother Methuselah's birth, openly discussing a mutual longing he shares with Dianne Feinstein – to ban private gun ownership (sorry if the wording momentarily led to an ugly mental image of that pair twisted into a carnal pretzel). However, Stark's working class district is littered with voters game enough to petition Pete to enforce the Constitution instead of his normal practice of using it for personal hygiene. One voter wrote to Stark about a gun control issue to which Pete misquoted an ancient Supreme Court ruling, apparently borrowing the spin directly from a Brady Campaign briefing document. When confronted about his legal larceny during a town hall meeting in Alameda, California, Stark stated, "I read a report once that said gun owners were compensating for small penises."

Pete cited a joke web site maintained by a Special Project Coordinator for PETA. Your tax dollars at work.

Stark raving madness aside, Pete's abuse of constitutional reality is illustrative of how the gun control industry spent decades inching public belief toward the notion that the phrase "the right of the people to keep and bear Arms shall not be infringed" meant that the right of people to keep and bear Arms could be infringed on legislative whim.

**The Lie of Mirrors:** Constantly stating the inverse of a fact in order to steadily remove belief in that fact.

Simple denial of a fact is a prerequisite to inverting public opinion. The simpler and more observable a fact is, the more bluntly it must be denied. "You don't have any right to own a gun." "Michael Moore loves America." "I did not have sex with that woman."

Inverting the common and enduring belief that the Second Amendment to the Constitution protects an individual's right to own a gun required incessant denial. From America's founding and well into the 1960s it was legal and common wisdom that the Second Amendment's assertion of "the right of the people to keep and bear arms" meant precisely that, despite a seemingly odd preface to this statement of a right. This inveterate belief was pervasive to the point that constitutional scholars had written nearly nothing on the topic. This is a peculiar plight in an industry whose motto is "publish or perish." The only amendment in the Bill of Rights on which less had been written was the Third Amendment, due primarily to the dearth of soldiers quartering in the homes of constitutional scholars.

Following several 1960s assassinations, the gun control industry initiated a denial campaign that made Osama bin Laden look like a rabbi. Recognizing that the Second Amendment was an impediment to prohibition, denial of a Second Amendment right was a tactical prerequisite. As long as elected officials had constituents who maintained the traditional understanding – that private firearm ownership was a protected right – then gun banning was anathema and impossible. Public opinion about the Second Amendment had to change and that required denying that such a right ever existed. This protected politicians willing to legislate against the civil right to shoot burglars, and in slightly less dire situations, politicians.

Politicians understand the essence of self-preservation. They merely decline to see the same necessity for the public.

During the age of disco and other horrors, a number of curious papers were published on the alleged lack of Second Amendment protections. Most of these academic dismissals had a pair of interrelated weaknesses – they rested nearly all arguments on the half of the Second Amendment that did not mention the right of "the people." They also ignored everything the Supreme Court had said about the half of the Second Amendment that *did* mention the right of "the people." These law journal jaw droppers focused on the irrelevant while ducking judicial precedents. This is the academic equivalent of being caught in bed with another woman, tossing the sheets over her head and asking your wife, "New hairdo?"

**The Lie of Magic:** Redirecting the attention of the public away from the core of the topic to complicated irrelevancies.

Second Amendment deniers created among themselves a doctrine of faith about the lack of a right in the second installment of the Bill of Rights. No degree of arguing the basics – such as the history of the Bill of Rights or elementary school English – could detour the gun control industry and their acolytes from a near-religious belief that one out of eight amendments protected the rights of states while the other seven protected the rights of people. Even the phrase "the right of the people" was decried as illiteracy penned by Madison, Jefferson and other rubes. Funded by the gun control industry, sitting professors of constitutional law – aching to make some real money for a change – managed to find a few law journals to peddle their prose and plant seeds of doubt that the "the right of the people" had any modern meaning. Their argument rested on the notion that The People were only allowed guns when participating in the militia, that the militia had been replaced by the National Guard, and thus nobody had a right to keep and bear anything more lethal than spit balls.

### The Lie of Shifted Terms: Inverting the meaning of words in order to invert an argument.

In reaction to intellectually atrophied academics who denied Second Amendment realities, several lawyers and professors published on the origins of the right to own fire sticks. This small set of obscure scholars were published in small and obscure legal journals. Their works went largely unnoticed because constitutional law experts only read journals published by prestigious universities from which they wish they had graduated. There were practical reasons for this. Reading into constitutional law is boring and tedious even for lobotomy patients. Multiplying this misery is the fact that most constitutional law scholars write like judges, creating dense, obtuse and painfully oblique prose that requires great attention or powerful medications. Thus, anyone interested in inquiries concerning the existence of a Second Amendment right missed the bulk of what was written to counter incorrect ideology manufactured by the gun control industry.

That was until a self-professed "liberal Democrat" and "card-carrying member of the ACLU" published the counter perspective in the Yale Law Journal.

Sanford Levinson committed three *pecco academia* when he published *The Embarrassing Second Amendment* in 1989. Foremost was publishing in a prominent law journal a well argued analysis that contradicted twenty years of constitutional mythology while explicating more simple truths. The second and more serious sin was writing an entertaining article with a grace and humor of prose that unintentionally mocked the stale, turgid, hypnagogic style of everyone else in the business. Levinson was despised by his abstruse colleagues in the same way that middle-aged husbands despise Brad Pitt – for making them look bad by comparison.

However, Levinson's cardinal crime was confuting in a major law journal the notion that people have a "right to keep and bear arms." With its wide circulation, many academics with too much time and too little income were exposed to their first deep reading into the Second Amendment. As a group they came to the realization that nearly nothing had been published on the origins of that bit of constitutional law. It was an open, green field – an untapped body of ore ripe for mining given the raging public debate on gun control. They had a subject on which they could research, write and publish to advance their careers, elevate their status and rise from being unknown to merely obscure.

In short order law journals were flooded with new explorations about the Second Amendment. Unlike many elements of law, the origins of the subject were well documented. Scattered through public archives – and compiled into an 800-page book in 1991 – was every mention of the relationship between guns and citizens in America as part of the discussion of the Bill of Rights. Notes from the Federal Convention of 1787 were spelunked. Federalist Papers and Federal Farmers were queried. Debating letters between founding fathers were dusted off. Newspaper archives were raided, Senate amendment votes were tallied, debates in the House were reprinted and a few Whigs were exhumed to testify.

A combination of the amendment's plain English, mixed with common sense and hundreds of new scholarly analyses of Second Amendment origins created a problem for the gun control industry, namely consensus. Near the millennial cusp, a review of literature showed that the ratio of peer-reviewed law journal articles favoring the individual right interpretation of the Second Amendment to those that did not was 30:1. Within constitutional law circles the individual right theory was called the "standard model." Even academics on opposing sides of most issues were aligning in defense of the standard model. Right-of-center Eugene Volokh of UCLA School of Law was certainly behind this theory. So was hard-left leaning Laurence Tribe of Harvard Law School. Even Yale's Akhil Amar – considered an academic's academic, though oddly he is worth inviting to cocktail parties – agreed. The weight of evidence (and an 1876 Supreme Court case) was so strong that in 2001 a Federal District Court ruled that the Second Amendment protected individual rights. The flimsy constitutional detour sign erected by the gun control industry was rapidly being shot full of holes.

So they bought a few more academics, a law journal and a symposium to go along with their future presidential candidate.

### The Lie of Loyal Opposition: Rigging expert analysis and generating media coverage of the same to mask the true consensus.

Like a malevolent bogy, the Joyce Foundation blipped onto the political radar screen. Confronted with a decade of crushing constitutional law research shifting the consensus of modern Americans toward the same consensus as The People who ratified the Second Amendment, the Joyce Foundation doubled down. Cynics claim the Joyce Foundation bought an edition of the Chicago-Kent Law Review outright. Then again only a cynic would claim that a Chicago-based political action foundation with a Chicago-based future president on the board could buy an entire issue of a Chicago-based law journal.

Cynics. Realists. The difference is vague.

In 1999, orchestrated initiatives concerning gun control were woven together. The Clinton administration galloped toward more gun control. Media and PR experts constructed the Million Mom March from vapor – even Gawd had more raw materials to work with. The Joyce Foundation – with Barack Obama on the board – gave a healthy $84,000 to the

Chicago-Kent Law Review which returned the favor by publishing a single issue of their tabloid in which all articles were about the Second Amendment, and none were aligned with the consensus "standard model." The journal accomplished this by importing Carl Bogus as editor (that is his real name, not a nasty moniker assigned him by his constitutional law peers). Bogus' neutrality on the issue is a bit foggy given that his *curriculum vitae* lists being on the boards of Handgun Control, Inc., the Center to Prevent Handgun Violence and the Violence Policy Center. When a law professor and adherent to the "standard model" asked to be included in the symposium, Bogus was quoted as saying, "Sometimes a more balanced debate is best served by an unbalanced symposium. I did not, therefore, invite anyone who I knew subscribed to the individual rights model."

The Joyce Foundation got a bargain. A mere $84,000 bought them a law journal and a human soul.

Yet the tide of scholarly research (as opposed to the purchased variety) was rising and the gun control industry found itself rhetorically gasping for air. A Federal District Court down south ruled that the Second Amendment protected individual rights. Meanwhile a Second Amendment case was pulled together up north to challenge Washington D.C.'s handgun ban. A critical collision was coming, one where the Supreme Court would be asked the nature of the Second Amendment, just as it had been in 1876. Despite their best efforts, the consensus among constitutionalists was against the Joyce Foundation, and the Supremes were likely to repeat their 1876 act.

So Joyce quadrupled their bet, buying an edition of the Fordham Law Review, lobbing lucre at the Stanford Law and Policy Review and bankrolling Ohio State University's "Second Amendment Research Center," the last of which was approved during Barack Obama's final Joyce Foundation board meeting.

Rats tend to flee sinking ships.

Gnawing at the collective and collectivist consciousness of the Joyce Foundation was Heller. Arising in 2003, the Heller case (previously called the Parker case) was inching its way through the courts. Specifically created to test both the Washington D.C. handgun ban and the origin of the Second Amendment, Heller created a conundrum for the gun control industry and the Joyce Foundation. Copious quantities of their cash had not derailed the academic freight train fueled by Sanford Levinson and other "standard model" advocates. Early amicus filings in the Heller case showed that an individual rights argument would be well represented, perhaps creating an insuperable summit as they had a few years earlier in that southern district court case (the Emerson trial, for those whose brains have not yet exploded from case law overload). The gun control industry sensed their heterodoxy was on the losing end of a long argument. They entered pure panic mode when the D.C. Circuit Court in the Parker/Heller case ruled that the Second Amendment *did* defend an individual right – the "standard model."  An appeal would take the case to the Supreme Court, and if those jaundiced justices proclaimed that the Second Amendment was a right of The People, then gun prohibition itself might be prohibited. The end game of the gun control industry would be heavily hobbled if not forever foiled.

### The Lie of Bluff: Stating a lie with authority to get the media to repeat your claim.

"The overwhelming weight of scholarly opinion supports the near-unanimous view of the federal courts that the constitutional right to be armed is linked to an organized militia," Dennis Henigan said with a straight face. As director of the legal action project within the Brady Center to Prevent Gun Violence, Dennis had no choice. When organizationally you are in a perpetual state of public denial, admitting to lurking fears and the weight of adversarial evidence would be damaging to the ego, the organization and your employment status. "The exceptions attract attention precisely because they are so rare and unexpected," said Dennis in reference to the "standard model" of the Second Amendment.

Naturally Dennis was preaching to the choir – the New York Times by name – an institution dedicated to any cause the left of Fidel Castro. Using logic less organized than a pot of spaghetti, The Times reported that "leading liberal law professors" were responsible for promoting the "standard model" of the Second Amendment, eroding an "almost complete scholarly and judicial consensus" against the same. They cited Tribe, and Amar and Levinson and studiously avoided Volokh, Hardy and Reynolds. They even interviewed the vaguely animated intellectual corpse of Carl Bogus who insisted, "Contrarian positions get play … Liberal professors supporting gun control draw yawns."

If the Joyce Foundation was near hysteria over the Heller case, their former Board of Directors member Barack Obama was more than merely concerned. In his eight years guiding grants for the foundation, Obama was aware and supportive of their attempts to revise constitutional history and influence the courts (Obama has gone out of his way to remind us that he once taught constitutional law, though his students are demanding tuition refunds). With Obama's Joyce Foundation grants keeping nearly every gun control organization afloat and financing medical professionals' amateur criminological work, Barack Obama was slightly antagonistic to the Second Amendment in the same way that Hitler was slightly antagonistic to Jews.

**The Lie of Action:** Making claims that contradict your past actions in hopes that those actions are forgotten and your future actions will not be predicted.

"... and how I have consistently spoken about my respect for the Second Amendment" was Obama's equivocation during the campaign.

Aside from partisan affiliations and suspect sanity, one other element unites Barack Obama and the always charming Congressman Pete Stark. Obama taught constitutional law and in that time surely encountered the major cases that defined American jurisprudence including the *Cruikshank* case of 1876. This case involved a group of post-Civil War black Republicans who were peacefully assembled and suitably armed, but none the less slaughtered by unrepentant ex-confederate Dixiecrats. Before the court were issues of both the First Amendment's guarantee of the right of The People to peaceably assemble as well as the right of The People to own guns to defend themselves against former confederates and their forcible Democrat takeover of courthouses.

Of interest to all constitutional scholars was the fundamental principle articulated by the Supreme Court in that case:

> The right of the people peaceably to assemble for lawful purposes existed long before the adoption of the Constitution of the United States. In fact, it is, and always has been, one of the attributes of citizenship under a free government. It "derives its source," to use the language of Chief Justice Marshall in 22 U. S. 211, "from those laws whose authority is acknowledged by civilized man throughout the world." It is found wherever civilization exists. It was not, therefore, a right granted to the people by the Constitution. The Government of the United States, when established, found it in existence, with the obligation on the part of the States to afford it protection ... The right of the people peaceably to assemble for the purpose of petitioning Congress for a redress of grievances ... is

an attribute of national citizenship, and, as such, under the protection of, and guaranteed by, the United States.... The right there specified is that of "bearing arms for a lawful purpose." This is not a right granted by the Constitution. Neither is it in any manner dependent upon that instrument for its existence.

In 1876, one hundred years into the life of the United States, the Supreme Court adopted the "standard model" for the Second Amendment.

Curiously, Pete Stark's problem came from citing the same case to deny the "standard model." Like his kindlier brother Satan, Stark can recite scripture for the purpose that suits him. He also can miscite case law for the same purposes. The letter Pete wrote that caused him to publicly align with PETA in defaming gun owners cited the *Cruikshank* case, though the selected extract was as exacting as a surgeon's incision.

A competent surgeon that is, not the one responsible for Pete's botched lobotomy.

The court ruled that "The right there specified is that of 'bearing arms for a lawful purpose.' This is not a right granted by the Constitution. Neither is it in any manner dependent upon that instrument for its existence. The second amendment declares that it shall not be infringed, but this, as has been seen, means no more than that it shall not be infringed by Congress." What Stark copied into his correspondence was "The right there specified is that of 'bearing arms for a lawful purpose.' This is not a right granted by the Constitution."

"So it's not surprising then that they get bitter, they cling to guns or religion ..." was Obama's fundraising oblation well before the Supreme Court decided the Heller case, confirmed an individual right to cling to guns, and sent Pete Stark in search of much-needed tranquilizers.

# Chapter 11: The Straw Men Straw Man: The Trafficking That Isn't

(how Michael Bloombergs lie)

It is a compelling visual. There is a Pagans motorcycle gang member, rocker patches blaring from his black leather vest. An MS-13 drug enforcer wears a "wife beater" t-shirt so acres of arm tattoos are fully exposed. A Gambino Family hit man quietly surveys the space, eyeing the other criminals with old-school disgust. In one place, in one room, their butts are planted on tastefully embroidered sofas and love seats, sipping white wine and "burping" plastic food containers.

"Tupperware® Parties for Criminals" was how the Violence Policy Center portrayed gun shows. Their prose violates the first rule of marketing – don't confuse your audience with mixed imagery.

Gun shows are unusual to everyone inside of Michael Bloomberg's office. With approximately 5,000 such shows every year and an estimated 75,000,000 attendees, they are not unusual to anyone else. Upwards of 15,000 people attend the bigger shows, and that excludes the NRA annual meeting which is such a gun owners' love-in that vice squads are put on alert. The only events more common than gun shows are hook shops financed by ACORN accountants or Nancy Pelosi's Botox injections. The mere existence of such frequent and widespread communal activity among gun owners made Senator Frank Lautenberg want to hide under the sheets, which Robert Byrd would have happily lent him providing that Frank returned them in time for the next cross burning.

The Violence Policy Center pitches their propaganda to the few Americans who have never ventured near a gun show, a rapidly shrinking audience given the rising rate of private firearm ownership. Common is the knowledge that the firearm trade has been heavily regulated since before Woodstock, so it is a bit difficult to spook the average voter about gun sales at gun shows. The same laws, background checks, paperwork, bureaucracy and taxes that licensed firearm dealers endure in their stores are suffered at shows. Which is why the Violence Policy Center, the Legal Community Against Violence and other Joyce Foundation-funded outfits talk not about licensed gun dealers but instead about beef jerky and luggage salesmen.

### The Lie of Inclusion: Including inappropriate people or organizations in a group.

Gun shows sell a lot of non-guns. For every display table with one or more firearms for sale, there are two without any, and for good reason. These non-gun vendors sell associated needs at gun shows. After all, as long as you are picking up that new Glock you might as well get a box of ammo (the cheap loads are over on aisle seven at Big Bob's Bullets), a holster (see Larry's Leatherworks on row four and get that lace-front bodice for the wife while you're there), a carrying bag for the Glock and bullets (the Saddle Pack luggage dealer is on aisle fourteen), a bumper sticker that insults politicians (Abdul's Batty Bumpers, row two) and a snack because all this shopping makes you hungry (Jerry's Jerky, "Best Dry Meat This Side of Hillary's Hide," aisle six). Better grab a can of the surplus gun oil ... you might need some lubricant after your wife puts on that leather bodice (Oli's Gun Oil and Adult Toys, aisle nineteen).

Handgun Control, Inc. loved to declare that "25-50 percent of the vendors at most gun shows are unlicensed dealers." Citing the same source, the Legal Community Against Violence claims "that 25 to 50 percent of gun show vendors are unlicensed." What the BATF report they cite actually said was "[Federal Firearm Licensees] make up 50 to 75 percent of the vendors at most gun shows." The rest sell luggage, beef jerky and petrochemical lubricants (for external application only, but who wouldn't want their wife to smell like a well cleaned Colt).

Gun shows are one of many gun control industry strawmen, which the dictionary defines as "a fabricated or conveniently weak or innocuous person, object, matter, etc., used as a seeming adversary or argument." The definition is rhetorically redundant for gun control mavens since they claim gun shows are a primary source for "strawman" purchases. Another definition for "strawman" is "a person whose importance or function is only nominal, as to cover another's activities; a front." In gun control industry parlance, these are people who buy a gun for someone else, allegedly an ineligible owner. The final definition for "strawman" is "a mass of straw formed to resemble a man," which inside of gun control debates can only describe Dick Durbin.

**The Lie of Union:** Connecting two or more unrelated elements that occur in proximity to create the appearance of a problem caused by one.

Lost in the manufactured confusion between baggage, beef jerky and bodices is the gun control industry's strawman. The concept of an "unlicensed dealer" was designed to create the illusion that people continually retail firearms without a license, something that has been expressly forbidden since Joe Louis knocked the taste out Max Schmeling's mouth. By classifying bumper sticker and luggage vendors as "dealers" at gun shows, and because they are not required to obtain a Federal Firearms License to sell tote bags and automobile decorations, the gun control industry coined a technically accurate phrase (50% of vendors are 'unlicensed') that generates the completely false impression – that most of the vendors at gun shows are rogue retailers peddling heat under the table and under the noses of law enforcement.

It is pretty clear what the Violence Policy Center is peddling.

### The Lie of Straw: Using a seemingly evil entity as a non sequitur point of argument.

Why would the gun control industry need to create this strawman? Such a clearly incompetent canard needs a purpose. As always the purpose is to pass legislation that conflicts with what voters really want, which from the rising rate of handgun purchases appears to be attending gun shows (no statistical data is available concerning demand trends for leather bodices and illicit gun oil usage). Yet data does demonstrate that gun shows are not a problem as far as violent crime is concerned. Number nuts at the Bureau of Justice Statistics decided to harass incarcerated inmates and determine how they came by their crime guns. Bureau busybodies report that fewer than 2% of these inmates purchased a piece at a "flea market or gun show." Other similar surveys of sleezballs showed the rate for just gun shows (sans flea markets) to be south of 1%. Clearly there is little connection between gun shows and criminals except in Michael Bloomberg's moonstruck microcosm.

"Because of the gun-show loophole," said a spokeschimp for Mayor Bloomberg, "we know that a criminal will take the path of least resistance."

The Brady Campaign provides even less clarity. Their gun show web pages proclaim "… unlicensed sellers are not required to do background checks, this loophole causes particular problems at gun shows which give these unlicensed sellers a guaranteed venue." Perhaps background checks for unlicensed beef jerky sales *are* necessary in a country where morbid obesity has become a competitive sport (beware Japan, America will soon dominate sumo wrestling!) and a "one bag of jerky a month" law might be in order.

Here we witness an unseemly extension for the illusion of unregistered retailers running revolvers through gun shows and directly into the hands of suspicious souls outside of MSNBC. Brady's web site continues the gun control industry con by associating thugs with bumper sticker sellers. "In most states convicted felons, domestic violence abusers, and those who are dangerously mentally ill can walk into any gun show and buy weapons from unlicensed sellers."

Did you catch the furtive fraud, the linguistic sleight of hand? Gun control industry artifice shifted one word, changing the concept of unlicensed *dealers* to unlicensed *sellers*. In most every state of the Union, private citizens can sell firearms to one another without the need of a license so long as they are not making a business of it. Dealers have licenses. "Unlicensed dealers" at gun shows sell accessories and promote new uses for gun oil. Unlicensed *sellers* are your neighbors. Three distinct groups of people – one of which has nothing to do with the buying or selling of firearms – are intermingled more freely than body fluids at a San Francisco sex club, venues where local law prohibits recreational use of gun oil.

Flexible farrago is essential to political fakery. It is nearly impossible to enact laws that harass your neighbors because you know your neighbors and know that you are next. Yet create the impression of faceless renegade retailers illicitly trafficking tools of carnage, and voters might look up from their favorite reality television show long enough to call their Congress critter. And if Americans ever want to abandon reality television, they can return to fiction by watching C-SPAN broadcasts of Congressional floor speeches.

Gun control industry literary larceny was designed for a backwards purpose. Once voters visualize uncontrolled trafficking of deadly items (like saturated-fat-loaded beef jerky) the gun control industry proffers their call to action; legislating away what they call the "gun show loophole" (the ironic element being that "loopholes" were originally slots made in fortresses through which shots could be fired in self-defense). Unlicensed *sellers* (a.k.a. your neighbors) are not required to keep dealer records because they are not dealers. Unlicensed *dealers* at gun shows don't sell guns. Yet in a world with nine-hour work days, two-hour commutes, kids' soccer games, in-laws, talking your wife into slathering on a coat of gun oil, and the rest of the stuff we call life, the average citizen has no time to pick apart these confusing semantic differences.

Civilian single-shot "assault weapons" are not military "assault rifles." Unlicensed "sellers" are not unlicensed "dealers." "Michael Bloomberg" is not a "sane human."

**The Lie of Linguistic Substitution:**
Using similar-sounding phrases to blur the distinction between the undesirable and desirable so the desirable is vilified.

Completely baffled? That was the gun control industry's intention, so let us walk through the primary points:

- Upwards of 50% of the dealers at gun shows sell gun-oil-flavored beef jerky but no guns.

- Citizens selling personal firearms are not required to have a Federal Firearms Licenses and go to gun shows, occasionally bringing a firearm they want to sell.

- Every other firearm transaction at a gun show is handled by a registered firearm dealer and the buyers endure federal background checks.

The fabled "gun show loophole" then involves not the 50% of gun show dealers who don't sell guns, but a handful of your neighbors who have an extra firearm that they wish to convert into cash, which they can then convert into a slicked-up, bodice-wearing wife. This also explains why the government reports that fewer than 1% of crime guns were obtained at gun shows – your neighbors are simply selling off their personal hardware, and typically trade with other law-abiding folk or sell to licensed dealers.

Curious then is the use of the word "loophole" to describe the situation. In legal lingo, loopholes are "a means or opportunity of evading a rule, law." Since legislation was mindful about the freedoms of non-criminal private citizens to buy and trade personally owned property, then no loophole exists. If a licensed dealer knowingly sells to unqualified buyers *anywhere*, including at gun shows, there is no loophole but a clear violation of law. If Larry's Leatherworks refuses to sell you a bodice for your wife then you need to stop buying her beef jerky because Larry has aesthetic standards to maintain.

The Brady Campaign and other cohorts in distorts are not dumb, providing we first remove Paul Helmke from the roster. The gun control industry is painfully aware that claims without apparent substantiation are highly suspect, and easily dismissed by people unwilling to sacrifice their neighbor's rights. Thus the gun control industry trots out government reports and distills from them incriminating sound bites that portray gun shows as the leading cause of death after beef-jerky-induced heart disease. A tactical advantage that the gun control industry obtains in this process comes from government criminological reports being slightly denser than Chuck Schumer and even more indecipherable. Few folk have the gumption to wade through reams of statistics or government-mandated unintelligible prose that competes with Sanskrit for the least understood language.

A case in point is where the Brady Campaign paraphrases an old Treasury Department report and in turn claims, "Gun shows are a major trafficking channel according to ATF, with an average of 130 guns trafficked per investigation, and over 25,000 firearms trafficked in total over one 17-month period alone." That is a lot of guns and a lot of guns per investigation, and very few of them were used in crimes. From the same Treasury Department report the Brady Campaign cites we encounter a few tidbits Sarah and Company studiously omit:

- "While a case review does not measure the full extent of the use of trafficked firearms by prohibited persons or in subsequent crimes ..." Translated from bureaucratic triple-speak into English, this report does not attempt to determine if any of the guns in these investigations are ever used for rape, robbery, murder or Philadelphia poll watching.

- Of the investigations, "No potential for charges" and "Insufficient evidence/unable to substantiate violation" constituted 45% of the cases Sarah cites. These cases were *investigations* and nearly half showed no crimes were committed or the evidence was so weak that charges could not be filed.

- "Half of the trafficking investigations involved at least one firearm recovered in crime." As the same Treasury Department routinely notes, guns *recovered* at crime scenes may not have been *used* in the commission of a crime, like when the local cops takes your pistol for a day after you wound a burglar, which occurs shortly before your neighbors buy you some beef jerky to thank you for your service.

It is enough to make you distrust the government, like everyone else does.

Being ever alert to their own effluvium, gun control demigods decided to buy a backstop to bolster this leaky government data. As always, when the gun control industry needs to buy bunko, they turn to the Joyce Foundation for funds and to colleges for cow plop. The tiny university town of Davis, California endures the unfortunate circumstance of being spitting distance from the state capital and the institutionalized irrationality that occasionally escapes. California's love/hate relationship with freedom has caused the state legislature to enact any number of chronically bad ideas, equaled only by the chronically bad ideas voters create through referenda. One such mistake is the Violence Prevention Research Program (VPRP), a four-person fallacy factory located in the U.C. Davis Health System – yes, another Joyce Foundation-guided group of doctors doing criminology research. It has been speculated that doctors pimping Joyce Foundation positions do so because there are no malpractice lawyers to worry about in criminology.

U.C. Davis' criminological malpractice is led by Dr. Garen Wintemute, who performs emergency medicine in Sacramento and who tortures students of emergency medicine at Davis. His web-based Violence Prevention Research Program résumé discloses no education or background in criminology, economics, statistics or any discipline involving numbers. Garen researches solo in the VPRP with occasional assistance from an epidemiologist and whatever recently sober undergraduates can be found wandering around campus.

This makes them experts on gun shows.

Many gun control industry members – a group which includes the British Medical Journal, a formerly respectable rag that published Garen's jest – proudly promote Wintemute's masterwork, whose elongated title includes the phrase "observational evidence" (this phrase, by the way, is as close to honesty as we can expect from the gun control industry). Garen's research involved surrogates strolling through 28 gun shows (0.5% of those held annually) unevenly spread across five states (1/10th of those in the nation) and observing your neighbors as they inspected and occasionally bought guns, leather bodices and quarts of gun oil. Being a health professional it is assumed that Wintemute nutritionally avoided the beef jerky vendors. However, Garen asserts that he *measured* the number of strawman purchases made at these shows, a set of figures amplified by the gun control industry and which ricocheted unchecked through the media. Indeed, when the report was first released, U.C. Davis invited the media into a teleconference and presented covert video of an alleged straw sale at a gun show.

Odd that the video seems to no longer be available on the U.C. Davis web site.

As exposed in the video, Garen's "observational evidence" involves making assumptions about the *intentions* of other people. Florida's 2000 presidential recount proved this is a concept more flawed than trying to talk your wife into a threesome. In the now not locatable video two men are seen at a vendor's table, one examining firearms with interest and the other standing behind looking as bored as C-SPAN viewers. When the more animated fellow identified a particular firearm, he showed it to the other man who nodded with academic approval. When viewed by anyone with multiple functional dendra, it appears that the first fellow is seeking confirmation from his more knowledgeable cohort that the product and deal offered were good ones.

Garen's "observational evidence" was that a strawman sale had occurred.

The difference between "observational evidence" and the authentic variety is more dramatic than the difference between suggesting to your wife that she wear a leather bodice and suggesting that her sister wear it; the primary difference being that "observational evidence" does not require obtaining the services of a divorce attorney. "Observational evidence" requires assumptions which vary depending on each observer's bias. Given that the Joyce Foundation was paying medical doctors to prove a criminological improbability about gun shows, "observational evidence" indicates that all of the researchers involved were thoroughly biased and borderline imbecilic (that too is a biased assumption, and one no more valid than those made by Wintemute team members). Indeed, Garen lifted his intellectual skirt when he reported, "The observer then monitored gun sales and collected *anecdotal* data, walking through the show in a non-patterned manner" (emphasis clearly not his).

Omitted in his methodology was anything resembling proof. No confirmed transfers of firearms were made to the second person. No proof is offered that the second person – the one who never received possession of the firearm – was ineligible to own one. No cops were called, no arrests were made and the only conviction was in a doctor's mind. In short, no evidence was presented – only opinion. And sadly, nobody's wife was videotaped slapping her libidinous hubby for lewd sibling suggestions. That would have been more illuminating than the U.C. Davis report.

"It's easier for a criminal to buy a gun at a gun show than it is for one to rent a car" was New York Mayor Michael Bloomberg's observational evidence in explaining why less than 1% of crime guns come from gun shows. "Gun shows are supposed to be places where sportsmen and collectors can find products at good prices, not havens for criminals and gun traffickers."

Buried in Bloomberg's bromide is an important question, one which the gun control industry declines to ask or answer: Why would a career criminal bother going to a gun show when they are on a first-name basis with their neighborhood underground dealers? Those pesky bean counters at the Bureau of Justice Statistics, once they finally let incarcerated felons get back to shanking and shower rape, reported that 39% of felons obtained their crime guns from street sources, and just as many bought, traded or stole them from family or friends. When 78% of crime guns can be found in your slum, why bother traveling to an event littered with cops and ornery NRA members?

For the same reason that Mayor Michael Bloomberg does not, namely being unwelcome and subject to arrest.

Bloomberg has taken the gun control mission as his own, and in the process created the Mayors Against Illegal Guns Coalition with a little financial help from the same people who brought you Dr. Wintemute's whopper – the Joyce Foundation (if you have yet to identify the common financial thread throughout the gun control industry, you might have the proper IQ to conduct criminological research for the U.C. Davis medical school). Uncharacteristically for an active arm of the gun control industry, Bloomberg's coalition puts the public interest at the forefront of their press releases. Bloomberg's web site glorifies their organizational kick-off meeting where "... senior officials from 13 cities in five regional states met in Atlanta, GA to discuss access to *accurate* data, *coordinated policing strategies*, and community engagement on gun issues."

Accuracy was Bloomberg's first victim. Unlike Michael, you will recall that of the 30,000 "gun deaths" each year, 56% are suicides. Since the misleading "30,000 gun deaths" sound bite has for decades been an open and well known issue, Bloomberg's insistence on accuracy is odd given that in his statement of coalition principles he writes, "Whereas: 30,000 Americans across the country are killed every year as a result of gun violence." Yes, suicide by gunshot is a violent event, but categorizing it as "gun violence" is inaccurate, and following up that assertion with "... we are duty-bound to do everything in our power to protect our residents, especially our children, from harm and there is no greater threat to public safety than the threat of *illegal guns*" is downright shady.

### The Lie of Clusters: Combining disjointed and emotional elements to obfuscate more basic fallacies.

Bloomberg's business is that of "illegal guns," the trade tool of common criminals. In one web page Michael seamlessly attaches these thugs to suicides – which are all but universally committed with legal guns – and to children, who are rarely victims of gun violence, providing we discount post-pubescent street gang members. However, we cannot discount the criminal element, like the four members of Bloomberg's coalition who have been under felony indictments, five more convicted of felonies, one who croaked from a heart attack before his trial was over (he was warned about that beef jerky) and another convicted of a violent misdemeanor.

Bloomberg's coalition is a bigger threat to public safety than illegal guns.

The top agenda item for the Mayors Against Illegal Guns Coalition is getting their mitts on federal firearm trace records. Police from all jurisdictions can already request that the Bureau of Alcohol, Tobacco, Firearms and Explosives (BATFE) look up the serial numbers on guns recovered at crime scenes, providing that the serial numbers have not been removed by a drummel tool, hand file, power drill or Dennis Kucinich's fretted gnawing. Each trace request is logged in a database that returns the last known retailer of the firearm. This repository of gun traces is tempting to the uninitiated who view it as a potential tool for identifying the retail source of guns used in crimes and to prosecute licensed gun dealers into oblivion.

Too bad the Bureau doesn't agree. The BATFE and others note that traces:

- Include guns found at crime scenes but not used to commit crimes. One such instance included a hobbyist who committed a white collar crime, and his collection of nearly 100 guns were all traced.

- There are many more guns used in crimes than are traced, which creates inaccurate statistical information.

- The date when the traced gun was retailed is not reported, and thus a gun sold 20 years ago in Alabama and recovered today at a crime scene in Seattle may have legally changed hands several times.

- Many wholesalers also have retail operations, but guns they inadvertently sold to improperly licensed dealers (yes, the government does occasionally make mistakes) are recorded as their own sales. One such wholesaler showed up as a top source for crime guns despite having a spotless retail store record.

Bloomberg's fixation on obtaining unfettered access to data that the federal government says has no statistical relevancy seems a touch misguided and Michael a little touched. Despite the Bureau's disclaimers, Bloomberg insists that his coalition "Oppose all federal efforts to restrict cities' right to access, use, and share trace *data that is so essential to effective enforcement*, or to interfere with the ability of the Bureau of Alcohol, Tobacco, and Firearms to combat illegal gun trafficking."

The *thud* you just heard were Bureau investigators collapsing in spasmodic laughing fits.

In his cudgeling New York style, Bloomberg decided to take the law into his own hands and completely bypass working with the Bureau and various local law enforcement agencies. Using fragile trace data and identifying a few Southern gun stores, Michael hired some private detectives to buy guns at those Southern shops and did not coordinate this activity with the BATFE (remember, the Coalition's web site say that they will "coordinate legislative, *enforcement*, and litigation strategies," but evidentially not *enforcement* sting operations). Often Bloomberg's private dicks were a paired man and woman, with the woman posing as the purchaser and the man advising on which firearm to obtain. When the gun store sold the woman a gun that the man advised she buy, Bloomberg concluded this "observational evidence" to be the commission of a crime.

Wintemute already demonstrated the value of observational evidence. "Men routinely advise women on what guns to buy," said one of the stung gun store owners, having previously encountered many couples buying his-and-hers hardware.

More serious than Bloomberg ignoring the BATFE's reservations about trace data accuracy are the crimes he committed by proxy and the ongoing investigations he may have disrupted. The Bureau was properly quiet on the subject of who in the Southern states they may have been investigating when Bloomberg's sting was revealed. Yet a Washington source told a New York newspaper, "A bunch of private eyes straight out of 'Barnaby Jones' run their own sting operation and all the real enforcement agencies find out about it on the day they are having a press conference? Not good. The goal is to lock up gun criminals, not file civil lawsuits with publicity stunts."

Bloomberg's uncoordinated efforts caused ripples throughout the law enforcement community. Being somewhat more familiar with guns, gun stores, strawmen and the law than Mayor Bloomberg, certain agencies saw through his coalition's end game. Since the average chief of police knows that federal trace records are inaccurate and unviable as targeting tools, they are in no mood to have trace data opened to disreputable individuals, like New York mayors. Bloomberg's Southern gun store escapades caused local, state and federal law enforcement agencies to spend a lot of time *not* catching gun runners, handling instead out-of-control mayors from cities with strict gun control laws. They were especially annoyed because it kept them from a common duty, patrolling gun shows, which in turn kept them from eating some really good beef jerky and ogling women in leather bodices.

The Fraternal Order of Police decided that opening statistically inaccurate trace records to Bloomberg's mayors and their hired private dicks would create long-term misery for jerky-loving cops. The FOP officially came out against opening traces and, as a byproduct, against Michael Bloomberg. While bloviating at a breakfast hosted by the Ladies Home Journal, Bloomberg branded the 325,000 cops and 2,100 chapters of the FOP as "one fringe organization."

**The Lie of Coalition:** Pretending that membership in an organization is popular and the ranks are swollen and stable.

Ignoring problems associated with the useless trace data, with the fact that almost no crime guns come from gun shows, with possibly illegal Bloomberg-sponsored sting operations performed by private detectives, and with the berating of one of the nation's largest police organizations … ignoring all of these, it is the Mayors Against Illegal Guns Coalition defectors, more than its defects, that are most worrisome for Michael. Like an endless stream of clowns serially falling out of a tiny automobile, many mayors have fled the Bloomberg Bunch after reading media reports on Michael's long-term objectives and assorted slanders. Adios Idaho Falls. Ciao Carmel. Adieu Anchorage. Cheerio Rio Rancho. Toodle-oo Oldmans Township. Sweet parting Williamsport. Godspeed Knoxville. Bye-bye Burlington. So long Sioux Falls. See you later … everybody, except the four coalition members under felony indictments, the five already convicted of felonies, another charged with domestic abuse, and the other fellow convicted of a violent misdemeanor – I'm sure Bloomberg will visit you often … in your respective cells.

# Epilogue: The Discussion That May Be
(how Everybody lies)

Will Rogers said, "If you ever injected truth into politics you'd have no politics."

That would be a positive change.

A Brady Campaign web site FAQ asks, "Is Brady a 'gun ban' organization?" and answers, "Brady believes that a safer America can be achieved *without banning guns* ... We believe that law-abiding citizens should be able to buy and keep firearms.... [T]here are certain classes of weapons that *should be out of bounds for private ownership*." They then itemize affordable handguns and recreational sporting rifles as items they wish to ban.

No wonder voters are a surly and cynical lot.

Nobody likes a liar, but each of us is one. Your lies may be of the little, white variety, like telling your kids about Santa Claus, the Easter Bunny or government fiscal responsibility. Your neighbor's lies may be confined to his tax returns. Every résumé is an exercise in narrative fiction. All expense reports should be titled "Utter Buncombe." Pick-up lines in cocktail lounges ... let's not even start that discussion (though there are some mighty poor pick-ups that surprisingly work). We accept a modicum of lying when the negative impact is limited. As Robert Heinlein suggested, non-endangering lies are necessary social lubricants.

Which is why political lies are crucifixion-grade offenses.

When America devolved from being a constitutional republic into a mere democracy, power shifted from the individual to his and her government. Tyranny of the majority became part of American daily life. Democracy made it possible for people to regulate the non-hazardous private actions of their neighbors. All they had to do was simply get a majority of neighbors throughout the nation to agree.

Therein lay the rub with us rubes.

When a majority of people want to cling to their guns and religion, Barack Obama and atheists are unable to inflict their will. When you want to raise your child and Hillary wants the village to do it for you, existing laws favoring parental prerogative must first be rewritten, which requires convincing most other parents in the country to surrender their parental powers. Drafting laws that remove individualism from individuals requires convincing 50.1% of the population that freedom is expendable.

This is where lying comes in. People prefer to control their own destiny. They may or may not be good at it, but millions of years of evolution and thousands of years of politics have taught people that self-determination beats the alternatives. Individualism requires a great deal of individual freedom, a fact our founders recognized, especially the founders who owned slaves. Determined not to live like their chattel, they constructed a system of government where the central authority had little, and whose primary job outside of diplomacy (which is a very refined form of lying) and war (which is the failure of diplomacy) was to protect individual rights. For more than a century the federal government sloppily did their duty, and aside from a little civil war and the lackadaisical intervention against Jim Crow and his brothers, Washington was barely competent enough to keep.

In the early part of the 20th century a few key Supreme Court decisions changed the very nature of the Constitution, making possible any form of political mischief. The gun control industry, which always existed but had previously confined itself to disarming minorities, was invigorated. Banning firearms became legislatively possible. All it would take was convincing 50.1% of the population that surrendering tools of self-determination – and survival – was in their best interest.

The people clung to their guns and kept their religion to boot.

As one judge said at the beginning of each trial over which he presided, "Let the lying begin!" With Americans unwilling to disarm, the gun control industry began fabricating falsehoods in order to achieve what it had been constitutionally disallowed. Fibbing was not confined to gun control. Each insurrection into the territory of personal freedom required canards. In 1913 when Federal income tax was reintroduced, the top tax rate was 7% and promises were made that the rate would never rise. Today the *bottom* tax rate is 10% and the top has been as high as 92%. Lyndon Johnson's crew promised that welfare would assist only the truly downtrodden, yet ballooned to where nearly 10% of the population is receiving some form of your financial assistance and about the same amount of your tax dollars. Fannie Mae and Freddie Mac – two sagging Depression-era milk sacks hanging off our obese Uncle Sam's chest, and who are arguably responsible for the Great Recession of 2009 – were proposed as limited entities, yet grew like cancers, acquiring half of all mortgage debt before imploding. Most modern legislative disasters began with such false promises.

Combined they cannot eclipse what the Brady Campaign utters before breakfast.

Recall the purpose of lying, especially while explaining to your wife the unfamiliar shade of lipstick she found on your collar. People lie in order to get what they cannot obtain honestly. Small lies like those commonly told in bars can earn small and transient benefits, such as getting a little nookie. Moderate lies can land jobs, leverage property debt, or keep your wife from filing for divorce after she finds an unfamiliar shade of lipstick on your collar. Big lies let people get away with murder. The safety valve is that the lies we tell one another directly are discrete, one-on-one deceits that limit the damage done.

Damaging an entire nation requires whoppers.

Hoodwinking 170 million registered voters takes audacity. It also takes non-stop effort and flooding the electorate with disinformation from every angle, through every medium and from all corrupt but otherwise seemingly reliable sources. It requires an all-out initiative, especially when asking people to give up something they cherish. Demand surrender of money and people resist. Try to take a child away and you can expect a violent backlash. Stealing a man's wife could be fatal, unless of course the man just endured a long argument over some lipstick on his shirt collar, in which case a fellow might just gift wrap his wife before shipping her off.

Asking most households in the United States to give up their primary means of surviving violent criminal assault will earn you an extended stay in a well padded room.

As long as we rely on the mechanics of democracy instead of the protection of a constitution, some set of fanatical fabulists will try to enact their Eden. When your paradise conflicts with their envisioned Shangri-La and you decline their offer to enlist, prepare for prevarication. In mere democracies your right to be left alone does not exist, and every ideologue with the means will lie through their welfare-financed dentures to encourage your neighbors to force you into participation and subservience. For people wholly and unholy drenched in their perception of a great society, no lie is too large to tell. Their ends justify your means.

Thankfully, things are changing and lying is becoming an unreliable tool.

It is amusingly painful to watch members of the old Fourth Estate. They have yet to realize that they no longer control the national conversation. In days gone by, demented and disdainful intellectual desperados like Dan Rather could report pure fiction without repercussion. In those dark days, you received your current events knowledge through three network news channels (NBC, ABC and CBS) and one or two local newspapers. Lack of variety in facts and analysis created a sterile and often inaccurate portrayal of political policy if not life itself. Though Ted Turner's accumulated sins remain unforgivable, politically aware individuals owe him gratitude for launching the first fulltime cable news network (which instantly sank to the same journalistic skid row as Dan Rather's old haunt). No news channel is utterly reliable or otherwise, but now instead of obtaining our 30-minute evening world view from one of three incestuous outlets, we have multiple televised perspectives. We even import and tolerate reporting from the BBC, watch with odd fascination English Al Jazeera, and suffer through C-SPAN when desperate.

Then, there is the Internet.

When a few million intelligent but bored individuals are given a unified platform for research, analysis and sharing, power shifts from the organized Fourth Estate to the unorganized Fifth. Much like the conflict between organized Red Coats and the unorganized American militia, slaughter is guaranteed. Granted, a great deal of homegrown manure covers the green grasses of the Internet agora. After all, we all lie. But large-scale lies are losing viability on a planet littered with unpaid yet highly motivated fact checkers. The Fifth Estate now holds the first four in check, and electronically pillories people in power who proffer perjury. Small lies start an email chain. Big lies get you a permanent YouTube video. The unwashed masses (that would be you Bubba) are actively inserting truth into uncomfortable places.

As an information-driven culture, we are going through early electronic growing pains. Democrats squeal when Republicans lie. Conservatives scream when libs fib. Libertarians smoke contraband Havanas while watching these groups slug it out, placing bets on which camp spills the most political blood. Hidden is a highly interesting aspect of our early amateur intellectual mayhem: Each partisan posse is actively *reading* what their opponents have to say. Twenty years ago only talking heads in well funded think tanks had the luxury of doing such research. Today bleary-eyed, pajama-clad activists lose sleep to study and respond to their opponents' talking points. They are voluntarily exposing themselves to the details of adversarial thinking. For now it creates anger and a lot of rude online commentary.

Over the long term it breeds understanding, perspective and a little bit of trust.

Missing from the mix is a formalized framework for discussing deception. Telling thick-skinned politicos that they are liars has limited effect. Showing the world that a lie has been told requires framing the accusation. That is why *Shooting the Bull* came to life – to provide that framework. To give those millions of blurry-eyed, pajama-clad cranks a classification scheme for explaining lies to their audiences. Putting Pete Stark's mug on YouTube is a start. Prefacing his fiction with an explanation of how he lies puts Marley-grade chains around his effete frame. With a *linga franca* of fraud, we can effectively brand liars and cast them forever in doubt and disfavor. We have the means to reduce, perhaps even eradicate political lying.

Now get busy and make the bums squirm.

# The catalog of canards condensed

Below are all forms of fibs, lies, canards, casuistry, flummery, tergiversation, artifice and tidbits of tarradiddle covered in the chapters you have just read.

**The Lie of Fear:** Creating a false sense of fear in order to motivate people to action while easing them past critical thinking.

**The Lie of Definition:** Using purposefully vague or misleading definitions to create political or legislative leverage, especially when it splits the opposing faction.

**The Lie of Intimidation:** Triggering instinctive reactions to create unfounded fears.

**The Lie of Omission:** Purposefully excluding information to inappropriately change beliefs about an issue.

**The Lie of Looming Catastrophe:** Using worst case scenarios, regardless of how remote, to instill a fear of uncontrollable danger.

**The Lie of Association:** Using invalid associations to demonize a person or position.

**The Lie of Lewinsky:** Forcefully making flat denials of observable fact to cast doubt in otherwise lucid minds.

**The Lie of Concern:** Demonstrating an insincere state of concern for others in order to achieve tangential objectives.

**The Lie of Camaraderie:** Portraying false associations with a person or organization to create an emotive bond.

**The Lie of Statistics:** The use of numbers that present misleading information and distort perspective.

**The Lie of Authority:** To speak with authority, though not fact, and by such presence keep others from questioning the information.

**The Lie of Context:** Showing either a small snippet alone, or a string of snippets together, to create a false impression of what happened.

**The Lie of Non Sequiturs:** Combining vaguely related, or completely unrelated, information to create a false impression or conclusion.

**The Lie of Invalidatable Conclusions:** Pronouncing with certainty what has never been and can never be proven.

**The Lie of Invalid Policy Comparisons:** Comparing two seeming similar policies so the rational effects of one are inappropriately associated with the other.

**The Lie of Big Databases:** Claiming that sufficiently large databases will instantly identify useful information.

**The Lie of Proportion:** Avoid showing relative proportions in order to avoid showing the weakness of an argument.

**The Lie of False Intents:** Proclaiming a false goal to mask one's real objective.

**The Lie of Historical Obfuscation:** Obscuring or marginalizing historical trends in order to lure people toward the same end.

**The Lie of Science:** Using weak or irrelevant studies by topic "experts" to convince people that greater minds have reached a valid conclusion.

**The Lie of Methodology:** Using inappropriate and misleading research methods to create ill-founded conclusions.

**The Lie of Incomplete Comparisons:** Examining only one aspect of a cause-and-effect relationship to create the impression of a single cause and effect.

**The Lie of Inappropriate Experts:** Using otherwise credible people without subject matter expertise to research or opine on a topic.

**The Lie of Picked Cherries:** Using selected studies, or selected parts of studies, to substantiate an invalid conclusion.

**The Lie of Mass(ive) Assault:** Generating a huge amount of convincing but inadequate "research" in order to make an issue appear to have "scientific consensus."

**The Lie of Universal Competence:** Using experts in one field of study to opine in a different field, and having their credibility conceal poor research.

**The Lie of Peer Review:** Using bands of researchers who share the same biases to review and approve suspect research.

**The Lie of Technology:** Asserting that one or another technology will correct a perceived social disorder.

**The Lie of Snowflakes:** Claiming that every unit of a mass manufactured product is inherently unique and will always remain that way.

**Lie of Concealment:** Promoting a seemingly benign policy to surreptitiously enact a malignant one.

**The Lie of Increments:** Claiming that only a small intrusion into private matters is planned, knowing it can be made infinitely more intrusive later.

**The Lie of Even Better Technology:** Insisting that failed technologies will or have improved while ignoring the inherent problem.

**The Lie of Business Acumen:** Making inaccurate claims about the limited impact to business and customers in order make a costly proposal sound reasonable.

**The Lie of Pantyhose:** Claiming that people's situations are similar enough that one-size-fits-all solutions work universally.

**The Lie of Legislative Salvation:** Assuring people that law by itself will cure a social ill.

**The Lie of Accountability:** Falsely assuring people that those charged with performing a duty will attempt to do so.

**Lie of Moving Sources:** Changing the claimed source or cause of a perceived problem when facts make it necessary.

**The Lie of More:** Insisting that more of the same will produce a different outcome.

**The Lie of Mass Micro:** Claiming that a law restraining the masses will control the minority who actually cause problems.

**The Lie of Distance:** Comparing places to which the average voter has never traveled to create a misleading policy analogy.

**The Lie of Selected Cells:** Selecting a small number (often two) points of reference to create a false comparison, ignoring the remaining combinations.

**The Lie of Exotic Divergence:** Contrasting two items without exploring everything that might cause their differences.

**The Lie of Limited Perspective:** Avoidance of exposing the big picture or long-range trends.

**The Lie of Vague Intentions:** Uttering ill-defined but popular objectives while striving for specific and unpopular goals.

**The Lie of Humanitarianism:** Appealing to people's hopes that aberrant human behavior can be post-processed, and later enforced, by government.

**The Lie of Slices:** Using a small slice of data to simultaneously obscure the reality presented by all the available data, and creating a false sense of blame.

**The Lie of Cost:** Using arbitrary and inconsistent definitions of cost to create a sense of a serious problem.

**The Lie of Duration:** Not exposing the duration of the topic in order to inflate or deflate the apparent cost, risk or benefit.

**The Lie of Blindness:** Willingly repeating factoids that have been disproven in order to perpetuate the myth.

**The Lie of Balance:** Avoiding exposure of the opposite assumption in order to avoid providing balanced perspective.

**The Lie of Unexamined Alternatives:** Examining only half of an obviously two-sided discussion to keep people from obtaining a full perspective.

**The Lie of Synchronicity:** Creating the appearance of mass, spontaneous mutual consensus to cause the public to believe there is an urgent issue to be resolved.

**The Lie of Mirrors:** Constantly stating the inverse of a fact in order to steadily remove belief in that fact.

**The Lie of Magic:** Redirecting the attention of the public away from the core of the topic to complicated irrelevancies.

**The Lie of Shifted Terms:** Inverting the meaning of words in order to invert an argument.

**The Lie of Loyal Opposition:** Rigging expert analysis and generating media coverage of the same to mask the true consensus.

**The Lie of Bluff:** Stating a lie with authority to get the media to repeat your claim.

**The Lie of Action:** Making claims that contradict your past actions in hopes that those actions are forgotten and your future actions will not be predicted.

**The Lie of Inclusion:** Including inappropriate people or organizations in a group.

**The Lie of Union:** Connecting two or more unrelated elements that occur in proximity to create the appearance of a problem caused by one.

**The Lie of Straw:** Using seemingly evil entity as a non sequitur point of argument.

**Lie of Linguistic Substitution:** Using similar-sounding phrases to blur the distinction between the undesirable and desirable so the desirable is vilified.

**Lie of Clusters:** Combining disjointed and emotional elements to obfuscate more basic fallacies.

**The Lie of Coalition:** Pretending that membership in an organization is popular and the ranks are swollen and stable.

# Some additional canards I could not cram into the book

The gun control industry is a busy body, and they have coughed up a few canards beyond the scope of this book and the endurance of the average reader. Below I have summarized some additional displays of their deception.

**The Lie of the Promised Land:** Promise of utopian outcomes with no conceivable method or means for achieving them, often to gain a smaller, incremental advancement.

**The Lie of Guilt:** Playing to a human's innate sense of guilt, motivating them into otherwise irresponsible action.

**The Lie of Distracting Terminology:** Injecting confusing and inconsequential jargon into a discussion to distract people from the simpler and more understandable issue.

**The Lie of Equivocation:** The use of a term which has multiple meanings to present a false impression of the issue (e.g., "Michael Bloomberg is a *man*.")

**The Lie of Minutia:** Presenting massive amounts of meaningless detail to distract people from focusing on conclusions or other important information.

**The Lie of Historical Vectoring:** Presenting one historical element as a proof of concept without presenting the full scope of historical pressures.

**The Lie of Obvious:** Stating that something is obvious in an attempt to prevent someone seeking information.

# Acknowledgements

Hillary Clinton once mistakenly said, "It takes a village to raise a child," conveniently ignoring that many mothers and fathers have done the task quite well without interference from Hillary's villagers. Even a large number of single parents have muddled through and produced children bordering on presentable.

Writing a book is a different matter, with the exception that final production induces pain that rivals childbirth and headaches more severe than those caused by back-talking teenagers. Such is the case with this work, and I would be unfit for presenting in public if I failed to thank a number of people who helped this project along.

First and foremost, I wish to acknowledge the fans and volunteers in the *Gun Facts* project. After many years of toiling away on my own, I opened the *Gun Facts* book project to anyone who wanted to pitch in. These volunteers have dug through criminological data, read boring government reports, watched the web sites of the gun control industry and encountered their own mind-searing pain by proofreading my dyslexic documentation. When *Gun Facts* grew bigger than lil'ol me, they volunteered to do what honest, patriotic people do – cowboyed-up and did hard work.

There is also a smaller knot of volunteers who fact-checked the final version of the book. This was a non-trivial undertaking since the sources for many of the observations herein were buried in my disorganized, cryptic and Bulgarian-based notes. These volunteers made certain that all my statements were anchored in something defensible and documented, which is more than we can say for any gun control industry organization or Keith Olbermann. Assuming that my fact checkers enjoy their privacy, I'll simply say thanks to Ken, Kim, Frank, Jeff, Ryan, Jack, Edward, ET, the other Kim, Dennis, Gil, George, Kris, Thomas and Al. If I forgot anyone, blame either my poor spreadsheet skills or a tragic lack of caffeine.

Another volunteer who deserves special thanks is Dale, a member of the legal profession and thus initially under suspicion. However, Dale volunteered to check the book for any passage that might inadvertently induce other lawyers to launch litigation over libel, slander or plain bad taste. Being well educated in such matters myself, I was (almost) certain that I phrased prose well enough to avoid spending an undue amount of time enduring members of Dale's profession. But Dale added diligence, giving me and my creditors a comfortable night's sleep.

Next a big nod to Alan Gottlieb, head of the Second Amendment Foundation, who granted an early endorsement of the book as well as some guidance in the publishing industry. Alan's only failing is that he is a perfect gentleman, which does not always work well in the warfare known as American politics, but this fault makes Alan a refreshing change in this world where debate is won by who can shout the loudest. In our meanderings I also fed Alan some pro-gun activist contacts in Latin America so we can start exporting the Second Amendment to the rest of the western hemisphere. And as long as I'm thanking Gottlieb's, a note of appreciation to Julianne Gottlieb for introducing me to Brian Patrick who I later mislead into writing a foreword for this book, and to Brian for adding academic gravitas with his kind words and flattering observations.

Another endorsement note of thanks goes to Wayne Allyn Root, who was not very happy at our first meeting (given his perpetual optimism and good nature, this says more about my affect on people than anything else). Being natural-born libertarians, it came to pass that Wayne and I were at the 2008 Libertarian National Convention, he running for the presidential nod and me a delegate from the formerly great state of California. When it appeared that Bob Barr (an NRA board member) would win the top spot, I twisted Wayne's wrist a bit and suggested he seek the VP role. His facial expression showed that this was clearly unappetizing given how hard Wayne had worked for the lead role, but five minutes later he was on stage with Barr and the two became the only 100% pro-gun ticket in that election cycle. His endorsement of this book means much to me, and I fear he will want a lot of my time in return during the next election cycle.

Many recurring displays of gratitude to Chris Muir of *Day by Day Cartoon* infamy. Muir is a childhood friend who, despite spending his more formative adult years in my absence, developed questionable and unsavory habits anyway. Yet he has done me more favors than any human should expect from another, including the caricatures that decorate this book and likely caught your eye. He and my cover layout artist (a reclusive, shy and irritatingly politically correct friend who craves anonymity) make me as presentable as humanly possible.

More so than anyone else, however, I want to thank every man and woman who has seen combat and worn a uniform of the United States military. Every grunt, all jarheads, each flyboy, every squid and all the coasties. I can write this book because you kept me and my country free.

Now, if somebody could explain that concept to Sarah Brady.

# About the Author

Guy Smith is a San Francisco-based writer, songwriter, political provocateur and resident wag.

To say Smith has led an eclectic life is akin to assuming that China is a little overpopulated. In various eras Smith has been a cowboy and a surfer (even on the same day), worked for NASA, held guru status in the computer industry and earned a dime as a marketing strategist. A Southern gent by birth and upbringing, Smith ambled from one coast to another, temporarily halting in Georgia, Florida, Virginia and California.

Politically speaking, Smith is a "libertarian with a foreign policy." As a member of the Sons of the American Revolution, he claims to have genetically acquired a predisposition toward freedom and enforcing the same, primarily by dressing down politicians in the process. He is on record telling a former Congressman, "Once elected, you're my employee and my whipping boy."

Aside from writing both non-fiction and fiction, Smith contributes Op/Ed pieces to major metropolitan newspapers (San Francisco Chronicle and the Oakland Tribune among others). He has published hundreds of magazine articles and appears with appalling frequency on talk radio programs. He has been an invited presenter and speaker at multiple Gun Rights Policy Conferences and the Libertarian Party national convention.

Smith is also the author of *Gun Facts* (www.GunFacts.info), the standard desk reference for debunking gun control myths which NRA News host Cam Edwards referred to as "indispensible." You can keep up with Smith's philosophical and comical observations at www.GuySmith.org.

Made in the USA
Lexington, KY
26 May 2011